Tho

The Failures and Greatness of an Ordinary Man

By Jonathan Sistine

Copyright 2016 by Jonathan Sistine

Published by Make Profits Easy LLC

Profitsdaily123@aol.com

facebook.com/MakeProfitsEasy

Table of Contents

The Failures and Greatness of an Ordinary Man 1

Chapter 1: Of Great Deeds and Ordinary Men 5

Chapter 2: A Long Shadow 10

Chapter 3: Natural Distinctions 16

Chapter4: Liberty, Equality, Fraternity 38

Chapter 5: The Other Women 58

Chapter 6: The Winter Pilgrim 71

Chapter 7: The Nature of Man 80

Chapter 8: Duty and Domesticity 90

Chapter 9: A Divided House 98

Chapter 10: A War of Words 111

Chapter 11: The Farmer's Son 124

Chapter 12: Crimes and Punishments 135

Chapter 13: Strange Bedfellows 149

Chapter 14: Triumphs and Tribulations, Part One . 160

Chapter 15: The Case of Thomas Jefferson and Sally Hemings 169

Chapter 16: Trials and Tribulations, Part Two 183

Chapter 17: A Failure of Ideals 192

Chapter 18: The Finished Legacy 211

Chapter 19: A Great Man 219

References 229

Chapter 1: Of Great Deeds and Ordinary Men

It is a fact of history that great deeds need not of necessity be enacted by great men. It follows that the enacting of such deeds cannot be taken as sure evidence of a man's greatness. The nature of the deed, the circumstances that formed its motive, and the durability of its outcome are all relevant considerations. So too is the nature of the man. Polymath, politician, and Founding Father Thomas Jefferson occupies the highest heaven of America's sacred pantheon, sharing space in the collective imagination with no less personages than George Washington, Benjamin Franklin, and Abraham Lincoln. Surpassing even these luminaries, Jefferson's achievements have been among the most influential, far reaching, and enduring of the past three centuries. The Declaration of Independence, the Louisiana Purchase, and the school of political thought engendered by

Jefferson's dominant inclinations have inspired generations of admirers to assert his greatness. But as is the way with persons of power and celebrity, Jefferson's virtue has been questioned almost from the moment of his ascendancy.

The central issue in this debate revolves around Jefferson's affirmation of universal rights to "life, liberty, and the pursuit of happiness," while he paradoxically controlled the lives and constrained the liberty of above 100 persons of African heritage enslaved to his estate. A visitor to Monticello, Jefferson's "Little Mountain", would have observed slaves employed in all manner of agrarian and manufacturing tasks. Men tilled, men and women harvested, children as young as ten removed harmful worms from the tobacco plants that were Monticello's cash crop. When there proved to be a surplus of child labor after Jefferson transitioned to the growing of wheat, the master commissioned the building of a nailery where the boys could work until age 16. The girls he set to weaving. Supervision was delegated to the hands of white overseers, as was discipline, which included the whipping of young boys.

In his unedited draft of the Declaration of Independence, Jefferson railed against the British imposition of slavery on captive African people. But so long as the labors of his own slaves turned a profit, he took no steps to temper his reliance on the system he criticized.

How are we to rationalize the Jefferson who rallied his nation to a cry for freedom with the Jefferson who kept slaves? To dismiss the worthiness of his ideas would be an adolescent response, one not tempered by an intellectually honest appreciation of human nature. Jefferson was a man both complex and conflicted. In acting his many roles, he demonstrated a hunger for success that did not always accord with the rightness of his endeavors. This hunger informed his evident hypocrisy on the slavery question. Yet this hunger also drove him to take political risks, to put forth supreme effort when the moment required it, and to moderate his sometimes radical views for the sake of national unity. He acted selflessly in times of trial and endured a series of personal tragedies that might have sunk a less self-possessed man into permanent despair.

Through it all he erred, and erred grievously. His failures were of a kind with his successes: grandiose and memorable. Yet they were not the failures of an evil man, a duplicitous man, or a zealot. They were the errors of a man who sees the world as he would wish it to be, but finds himself unable to bring about his vision. They are the failures, in short, of an ordinary man. Brilliant to the point of prescience, Thomas Jefferson embodied the best qualities of the Enlightenment and brought to birth a nation built on its principles. His trespasses, even those committed against doctrines to which he pledged his passionate devotion, should not obscure his fidelity to a sacred ideal. The ability to exercise free will, benignly and governed by dictates of reason, was a right he sincerely believed belonged to every person by reason of birth.

What held him back from bestowing that gift on persons in his power? To understand this omission it is necessary to understand the larger context of Thomas Jefferson's world. The challenges he faced were unique to his time, and the way he confronted those challenges was unique to his person. An examination of Jefferson's life and mode of thought will do much to inform our understanding of his successes and failures. It may also serve to broaden our concept of greatness.

Chapter 2: A Long Shadow

Physically powerful, Peter Jefferson was a true frontiersman. While his son Thomas eventually grew into a tall and vigorous man, Peter's exertions were a world apart. *Aside from a modest inheritance of slaves and a more generous one of land, Peter Jefferson was a self-made planter. Like George Washington, he was a military man, serving in the Virginia militia. And, like Washington, he practiced the trade of a surveyor, embarking on long expeditions through trackless, difficult country, in constant danger from weather, terrain, beasts and men.* One year after Thomas's birth in 1743, he embarked on one such expedition, scaling portions of the Alleghenie mountain range en route to the source of the Potomac, where his partner, Thomas Lewis, placed the original Fairfax Stone. [1] The later Fry-Jefferson Map, which was included in *A Map of the Inhabited Part of Virginia containing the whole Province of Maryland, with Part of Pensilvania, New*

Jersey and North Carolina, published in 1753, was used as a source for John Mitchell's A Map of the British and French Dominions in North America, considered definitive at the time of the signing of the Treaty of Paris 1783. [2] When at home, Peter Jefferson served as a justice of the peace and, later, as sheriff of Goochland, a Virginia county settled by himself and his brother-in-law, William Randolph.

The influence of Peter Jefferson on his son's life was in some ways arrested by his early death in 1757, at the age of forty-nine. This was the first great tragedy of young Thomas's life. One result of this loss was the mythologizing of Peter's physical prowess. He was said to have torn down a derelict shed with his bare hands and tipped upright two bales of tobacco weighing 1000 pounds each. This superhuman quality must have left its impression on his son's mind. An avid horseman, Thomas Jefferson later advised his son-in-law to devote "not less than two hours" every day to exercise, regardless of the weather. [3]

What influence did physical vigor have on the mind of the philosophical Jefferson? Certainly his love of rural living was much influenced by long walks through the Virginia countryside. Approaching his eightieth year he still enjoyed riding his horse up to 20 miles a day. Without reading and riding, he once wrote, he did not wish to live. [4] These twinned passions, representing the pleasurable exertion of mind and body, forged a link to the past that Jefferson cherished. In books he could be transported to ancient Greece or Rome, or into the nostalgic fantasies of Don Quixote. Exercise of the body grounded him in both a more ancient past – the history of mountains – and simultaneously offered communion with the vanished shade of his father.

But it was books that absorbed the majority of his time. Jefferson was an eager student, mastering Latin and Greek, in which he read the great works of the classical age. His particular favorites were the epics of Homer. He spurned Plato, particularly despising the Platonic influence on nominally Christian religions. Though he considered himself a Christian in the sense that he admired and advocated the moral teachings of Christ, he had little use for the organized trappings of worship and a deep-seated animosity towards priestly authority. Priests and kings, in the mind of Jefferson, were equally to be suspected of suppressing liberty.

While the status of Peter Jefferson as a mythic figure in his son's life is easy to intuit, the role Jane Jefferson played is less clear. Chiefly this is due to the lack of correspondence between mother and son. Their letters may have been destroyed when the family home at Shadwell was destroyed by fire in 1770. The lady herself died six years later. She is all but absent from Thomas Jefferson's writings. Did he find the subject of her life and influence too painful to write about after her loss? Were the two eternally at odds, perhaps embroiled in a rivalry over headship of the household after Peter's death? No reliable source has yet been found that definitively answers these questions.

Death was a frequent visitor to the Jefferson household, often marring periods of life when Thomas had reason to be the most happy. In July of 1765, his sister Martha was married to Dabney Carr, the dear friend and fellow student about whom he later wrote, "his firmness was inflexible in whatever he thought was right: but when no moral principle stood in the way, never had man more of the milk of human kindness, of indulgence, of softness, of pleasantry in conversation & conduct." [5] Ever desirous of drawing his friends close, Jefferson was immensely pleased by the union. His happiness was soon arrested when his older sister, named Jane after her mother, died on October 1. Brother and sister had been fond companions. Both loved nature and delighted in taking long walks together through the woods. Thomas was an accomplished violin player, and would play for Jane as she sang hymns. Her loss grieved him deeply, its operations being recalled by his surviving siblings and related to the grandchildren.

Many more bereavements were to follow. Surely it is not surprising that a man who endured so much grief became famous for his philosophical outlook. Having borne so heavy a burden from a young age, is it any wonder that he longed for a better, freer world?

Chapter 3: Natural Distinctions

But to whom would that world belong? That question lies at the heart of a Jeffersonian understanding of the world. He was a keen student of history, understanding its tendency to recur. In this study, the abuses of absolute power were impossible to overlook. The English Civil War and its aftermath, culminating in the Glorious Revolution of 1688, was recent enough to show the trend of modern thought towards investing power in the populace, rather than in the monarch. It was also instructive of the failures of young democratic governments. Thomas Jefferson was well aware of the legacy that the American colonies would be taking on by demanding their independence from the British crown. He must have felt the weight of ages pressing down as he witnessed the changes that would bring about revolution.

In his first Inaugural Address, Jefferson acknowledged that, "some honest men fear that a republican government cannot be strong, that this Government is not strong enough". This notion was certainly not fanciful. The United States was a new experiment, but of a sort that had been tried before. The rise and fall of the Roman republic was one cautionary tale, England's parliamentary struggles another. But the cause of personal liberty was worth its struggle. "[W]ould the honest patriot, in the full tide of successful experiment, abandon a government which has so far kept us free and firm," continued the new President, "on the theoretic and visionary fear that this Government, the world's best hope, may by possibility want energy to preserve itself?" [6] His bold statement that the government, not just the nation or its ideals, was "the world's best hope", reflects an optimism at odds with the views of many of his contemporaries.

Long before his executive ascendancy, Jefferson's faith in the American ideal was tested. His upbringing as a Virginia planter, part of a self-made aristocracy defined by its pioneer spirit, made him uniquely sensitive to the burdensome obligations imposed by the mother country. The influence of Enlightenment idols, such as John Locke and Isaac Newton, prepared his mind to regard the struggles of the colonists against their remote masters in the larger context of the struggle between reason and totalitarianism. At William & Mary College, where Jefferson enrolled in 1760, he was thrown into a circle of intellectual giants that cleared a path for the budding scholar. Men like Dr. William Small, who taught Jefferson mathematics as well as ethics, enlarged his worldview. Thanks to Small's introduction, Jefferson became a frequent guest at the palace of the Lieutenant Governor of the colony of Virginia, Francis Fauquier. Fauquier provided Jefferson with an insider's view of English colonial politics. The association with Fauquier may also have deepened Jefferson's appreciation for the sciences, of which the Governor was an enthusiast. It was the fourth member of

Fauquier's favored table who had the most opportunity to mold the young Thomas Jefferson's thinking. A prominent lawyer, George Wythe took Jefferson under his wing, encouraging his legal pursuits. Their friendship would endure until Wythe's death in 1806.

Jefferson's inclination towards civic action came at an unsettled time in America. The Seven Years' War (1756-1763) between Britain and France, in which both sides being bolstered by Indian allies, saw an enlargement of British military presence in the colonies. It also saw an enlargement in British expenditure in colonial defense. To offset this expense, approximately 10,000 redcoats were garrisoned in the colonies, and lands west of the Appalachian mountains were forbidden to white settlers, per the Proclamation of 1763. Before the war, the British crown had taken no definite steps to apportion western lands, so this change struck the colonists, especially the frontier-minded Virginians, as an aggressive reversal. To the colonists, the west was a vast canvas on which they hoped to paint their fortunes, and the unrestricted possibilities it represented held much romantic appeal. The notion that the king would exercise his authority in this new way, carving up territory to which they felt inwardly a natural right, was abhorrent.

More abhorrent still were the new taxes imposed by London. The Sugar Act of 1764 proved unpopular for reasons illustrative of the trials to come. Though the act cut by half the import duty on molasses, it provided for enhanced enforcement that curbed the (sometimes illegal) free market activities of the colonial traders and manufacturers, as well as adding taxes on goods including coffee, pimiento, and some wines. Markets in several non-British ports were effectually closed to the colonies. An avid drinker of both coffee and Madeira wine, Jefferson was personally inconvenienced. Spurred on by George Wythe, the Virginia House of Burgesses sent a resolution of Parliament in

1764, protesting in advance of the passage of the similar, and more notorious, Stamp Act.

Jefferson was witness to the furor incited by the Stamp Act's passage. In 1765 he watched Patrick Henry take the floor to issue a declamation so fiery, it caused the Speaker of the House to caution him against speaking treason. Jefferson's own term in the House began in 1768, when he was elected as the representative from Albemarle county. Taxation was once again the issue du jour. Parliament had lately passed the Townshend Acts. Would Virginia join their sister colony of Massachusetts in protest? Inside of ten days after Jefferson's arrival, the House was dissolved by Francis Fauquier's successor, Lord Botetourt. Reconvening in the Raleigh Tavern, the representatives agreed to a general boycott of British goods.

It is tempting to imagine Jefferson's education and early career as a period of uninterrupted scholarly devotion – Jefferson claimed to study

15 hours a day – but the course of a young man's progress is never so smooth. After an attempt at courtship lasting at least two years came to a frustrating end, Jefferson wrote to a friend who had counseled him to make speedy arrangements to marry, "No, thank ye; I will consider of it first. Many and great are the comforts of a single state, and neither of the reasons you urge can have any influence with an inhabitant and a young inhabitant too of Wmsburgh. For St. Paul only says that it is better to be married than to burn. Now I presume that if that apostle had known that providence would at an after day be so kind to any particular set of people as to furnish them with other means of extinguishing their fire than those of matrimony, he would have earnestly recommended them to their practice." [7] Here he alludes to 1 Corinthians 7:9, as rendered in the King James Bible, "But if they cannot contain, let them marry: for it is better to marry than to burn." Historians have long debated what Jefferson meant by "other means of extinguishing their

fire". Did he perhaps refer to the not-unheard-of practice of white slave owners taking sexual advantage of their slaves? Might he have considered his elevated social standing to be license to intimate relations with women of a lower class?

This latter suggestion seems unlikely. Surely no man who knew his Bible would have expected Paul to be unaware of the tradition among early Israelite kings of taking on concubines. Paul's audience, per verse 8, is "the unmarried and widows", which doubtless included wealthy men in a financial position to emulate such a practice, and women of lesser means who might have been tempted to enter into the arrangement from the other direction. Jefferson gives the scriptural admonition the most humanist interpretation possible. He suggests that the apostle is counseling his audience on how to put an end to a painful human experience – unrelieved sexual urges – and makes no allusion to the moral dimension. That marriage might be a compromise preferable to sin seems not to be an issue contemplated by the young thinker. Having burned, he is pleased to have found a means to quench his flame. However coy Jefferson's reading, his pretending ignorance as to authorial intent would have been rhetorically inappropriate, particularly given that he is here responding to his friend's advocacy of the quotation. His "other means" must refer to a remedy unavailable to people of St. Paul's time and culture.

While slavery was common in ancient Roman society, there were features of slavery as practiced in the colonies that may have set it apart in Jefferson's mind. A Roman slave was typically a person from a conquered nation, or one acquired through piracy. Slavery was primarily a legal status, with a freed slave being permitted the same rights and privileges as other free persons, including the right to vote. Race was not a deciding factor. American slavery differed by being was defined in terms of race and religion. A Virginia colonial law of 1682 stated,

It is enacted that all servants. . . which [sic] shall be imported into this country either by sea or by land, whether Negroes, Moors [Muslim North Africans], mulattoes or Indians who and whose parentage and native countries are not Christian at the time of their first purchase by some Christian. . . and all Indians, which shall be sold by our neighborign Indians, or any other trafficing with us for slaves, are hereby adjudged, deemed and taken to be slaves to all intents and purposes any law, usage, or custom to the contrary notwithstanding. [8]

A popular justification of the time was that "Negroes, Moors, mulattoes or Indians" benefited from forced conversion, but this quickly fell apart once children were born into enslaved Christian families. Certainly by Jefferson's time, the prevailing view was that non-white races were inherently inferior. The necessity of this belief on the part of the slave owner is obvious. No other justification can co-exist with his claims to civilization.

In his *Notes on the State of Virginia*, published 1782, Jefferson laid out his argument for freeing and deporting African slaves. In answering the question of why freed slaves could not be integrated into a mixed American society, he acknowledged that among the reasons were, "deep rooted prejudices entertained by the whites" and "ten thousand recollections, by the blacks, of the injuries they have sustained". To this list he added, "the real distinctions which nature has made", concluding that any attempt at integration must end with the extermination of one or the other race. What follows is an appallingly bigoted recitation of white virtues when compared to black wretchedness. The beauty of pale skin and straight hair are lauded, and the black woman's figure subjected to insult. The writer goes so far as to say that blacks themselves prefer white looks, and notes the "preference of the Oranootan for the black women over those of his own species". [9] More telling than this appeal to his readers' aesthetic sense is Jefferson's assertion of intellectual, emotion, and artistic inferiority.

They are more ardent after their female: but love seems with them to be more an eager desire, than a tender delicate mixture of sentiment and sensation. Their griefs are transient. Those numberless afflictions, which render it doubtful whether heaven has given life to us in mercy or in wrath, are less felt, and sooner forgotten with them. In general, their existence appears to participate more of sensation than reflection. ... Comparing them by their faculties of memory, reason, and imagination, it appears to me that in memory they are equal to the whites; in reason much inferior, as I think one could scarcely be found capable of tracing and comprehending the investigations of Euclid; and that in imagination they are dull, tasteless, and anomalous.

Though asserting that his subjects are more gifted in raw musical talent than whites, possessing "accurate ears for tune and time", he continues:

Misery is often the parent of the most affecting touches in poetry. Among the blacks is misery enough, God knows, but no poetry. Love is the peculiar oestrum of the poet. Their love is ardent, but it kindles the senses only, not the imagination.

He then proceeds to dismiss extant black poetry as "below the dignity of criticism". In short, Jefferson's thesis is that blacks are, even more than Indians and other despised races, unworthy of consideration as full human beings. For evidence he looks to his own artistic sense, judging blacks as inferior because none in his sphere of knowledge has spontaneously come to an immaculate revelation, expressed in sweeping poetical terms, of Greco-Roman philosophy.

Plainly, the Thomas Jefferson of 1782 was a Southern, white, land-owning man of his time. His compassion towards enslaved persons was the compassion a man might have for a domestic beast he has seen badly used. More to the point, it was the compassion a man might have for a dog, whom after taking a beating, growls and snaps and drags at its leash. The man may feel ashamed at the dog's ill treatment, but he will not move at once to set it free. Rather he will remove it, taking it some safe distance from his home and family. He will lead it away, mounted on horseback and armed against attack. Only when he is sure he has the advantage over it will he set about freeing the animal, and even then, should it threat and howl and snap at the heels of his charger, he will, reasonable man that he is, set his compassion aside to blow its brains out.

In light of these thoroughly demeaning arguments, is it difficult to imagine that

Jefferson saw a difference between taking sexual advantage of a slave and engaging in sexual acts with a woman of his own race? As a young man, driven by sexual appetites and unsuccessful in his attempt at wooing, he may have been tempted to embrace the winked-at practice of sating such appetites with supposedly sub-human partners. In later life, he evidently clung to the belief in white supremacy, even in the face of evidence from persons of color who rose above economic and political disadvantages to make artistic and scientific contributions to society.

One such contributor was Benjamin Banneker, a free black from Baltimore County, Maryland. The son and grandson of mixed-race couples, Banneker was a keen student of mathematics and astronomy. Like Peter Jefferson, he also worked as a surveyor, accompanying Major Andrew Ellicott on an expedition to scout the boundaries of the Territory of Columbia, future capitol of the nation. In 1792, Banneker published his *Pennsylvania, Delaware,*

Maryland and Virginia Almanack and Ephemeris, detailing his calculations for certain astronomical events and their impact on agriculture, with additional content of a literary interest. Banneker sent his almanac along with a letter to Thomas Jefferson, who was then serving as Secretary of State. In his letter, which was published in the 1793 edition of the almanack, Banneker challenged Jefferson's assertions as to inferiority of the black race and asserted his confidence that the revolutionary author would view the plight of the enslaved with dissatisfaction. [10]

Sir, if these are sentiments of which you are fully persuaded, I hope you cannot but acknowledge, that it is the indispensible duty of those, who maintain for themselves the rights of human nature, and who possess the obligations of Christianity, to extend their power and influence to the relief of every part of the human race, from whatever burden or oppression they may unjustly labor under; and this, I apprehend, a full conviction of the truth and obligation of these principles should lead all to. Sir, I have long been convinced, that if your love for yourselves, and for those inestimable laws, which preserved to you the rights of human nature, was founded on sincerity, you could not but be solicitous, that every individual, of whatever rank or distinction, might with you equally enjoy the blessings thereof; neither could you rest satisfied short of the most active effusion of your exertions, in order to their promotion from any state of degradation, to which the unjustifiable cruelty and barbarism of men may have reduced them. [11]

Jefferson's response was brief. After thanking Banneker, he wrote,

Nobody wishes more than I do, to see such proofs as you exhibit, that nature has given to our black brethren talents equal to those of the other colors of men ; and that the appearance of the want of them, is owing merely to the

degraded condition of their existence, both in Africa and America. I can add with truth, that nobody wishes more ardently to see a good system commenced, for raising the condition, both of their body and mind, to what it ought to be, as far as the imbecility of their present existence, and other circumstances, which cannot be neglected, will admit. [12]

It is difficult to read this passage as anything other than insulting, to Banneker and his race, but this is partially the fault of modern prejudice, rather than Jefferson's own. His desire to "see such proofs as you exhibit" sounds insincere, knowing as we do that Jefferson the visionary, statesman and president failed in his lifetime to make any substantial contribution to the abolitionist cause. His own writings give another view.

"I am happy to be able to inform you that we have now in the United States a negro, the son of a black man born in Africa, and of a black woman born in the United States, who is a very respectable Mathematician," Jefferson wrote to his fellow political philosopher, the Marquis de Condorcet, who was himself an accomplished mathematician. "I procured him to be employed under one of our chief directors in laying out the new federal city on the Patowmac, and in the intervals of his leisure, while on that work, he made an Almanac for the next year, which he sent me in his own handwriting, and which I enclose to you. I have seen very elegant solutions of Geometrical problems by him. Add to this that he is a very worthy and respectable member of society. He is a free man. I shall be delighted to see these instances of moral eminence so multiplied as to prove that the want of talents observed in them is merely the effect of their degraded condition, and not proceeding from any difference in the structure of the parts on which intellect depends." [13] Here we see Jefferson appealing to Condorcet as one scientist to another. The "want of talents" he perceives in African people is an "effect of their degraded condition", e.g. their poverty and lack of a Western education, according to Jefferson's hypothesis. The discovery of Banneker is a vital clue as to its validity. Why then, was Jefferson not persuaded?

Some years after Banneker's death in 1806, he expressed to a friend his doubts about Banneker's mental abilities. He suspected that Ellicot had aided in the preparation of the almanacks in an attempt to inflate his neighbor's reputation. An interesting passage occurs at the end of this letter. After mentioning criticism he had received from another defender of black equality (the purpose of the letter was to comfort his friend after a negative review of a book of poetry from the same critic), Jefferson insisted that "it was impossible for doubt to have been more tenderly or hesitatingly expressed than that was in the Notes of Virginia, and nothing was or is farther from my intentions than to enlist myself as the champion of a fixed opinion". [14] That blacks were mentally inferior to whites was a belief he had adopted not without doubt, and one he did not express eagerly, or so he claimed. More telling is his assertion that he did not wish to be the champion of this idea. He had already made himself the champion of a more general liberty, the advocate of a new relationship between government and governed. Working out the particular application of his sacred principles to Africans, mulattoes, or Indians, either in the direction of expanded or contracted liberty, was a matter he wished to leave to other men.

Clearly, Jefferson was a man of rigid convictions. The tragedy of these convictions was that he used them to rationalize the miserable condition of fellow human beings. He might have argued that he did all he was able to do in life. As a Virginia legislator he proposed laws that would have made it easier for owners to emancipate their slaves, a failed attempt to remove a hurdle to abolition. But his argument is undercut by the personal benefit he derived from preserving the status quo. Slave trading, in which he occasionally indulged, was profitable, and slave farming kept Jefferson's family fed. It was one thing to deliver his fellow colonists from obligations to a transatlantic crown, another to destroy the lifestyle that fitted him like a fine suit.

Chapter 4: Liberty, Equality, Fraternity

From the moment he entered the Virginia House of Burgesses in 1769 until the end of his second term as President in 1809, Thomas Jefferson was at the center of a great experiment, not only in American liberty, but in the liberty of all literate, land-owning people. In 1776 he was given the singular honor of drafting the document that announced America's withdrawal from the authority of the British crown. Prior to 1776, he was known chiefly as the author of *A Summary View of the Rights of British America*, a tract prepared for the First Continental Congress in 1774. It was essentially a legal opinion arguing that American colonists held the right of ownership in their land, having undertaken its defense themselves. Though the congress rejected the more radical arguments of the radical Jefferson, its circulation in major cities made him a celebrated name. The Second Continental Congress, inspired by Thomas

Paine's popular *Common Sense* pamphlet, determined to announce their demands boldly. On June 11, 1776 they appointed a committee, including John Adams and Benjamin Franklin, to create a draft. Adams recommended adding Jefferson to the committee, since they needed a delegate from the large and powerful Virginia Colony. Asked to take up the task of writing himself, Adams substituted his Southern associate.

The Congress debated elements of Jefferson's draft for two agonizing days, cutting its most inflammatory language. The Declaration of Independence that remained was Jefferson's pared down essence, stating the case for secession as equitably as possible. The edits infuriated Jefferson, who called them butchery.

We hold these truths to be sacred & undeniable; that all men are created equal & independent, that from that equal creation they derive rights inherent & inalienable, among which are the

preservation of life, & liberty, & the pursuit of happiness; that to secure these ends, governments are instituted among men, deriving their just powers from the consent of the governed; that whenever any form of government shall become destructive of these ends, it is the right of the people to alter or to abolish it, & to institute new government, laying it's foundation on such principles & organizing it's powers in such form, as to them shall seem most likely to effect their safety & happiness.
[15]

The differences are jarring, so familiar are we with final form. Benjamin Franklin suggested "self-evident" in place of "undeniable". More consequential is the omission of Jefferson's accusation that King George III is responsible for slavery in the American colonies.

he has waged cruel war against human nature itself, violating its most sacred rights of life & liberty in the persons of a distant people who never offended him, captivating & carrying them into slavery in another hemisphere, or to incur miserable death in their transportation thither. This piratical warfare, the opprobrium of infidel powers, is the warfare of the CHRISTIAN king of Great Britain. determined to keep open a market where MEN should be bought & sold, he has prostituted his negative for suppressing every legislative attempt to prohibit or to restrain this execrable commerce: and that this assemblage of horrors might want no fact of distinguished die, he is now exciting those very people to rise in arms among us, and to purchase that liberty of which he has deprived them, by murdering the people upon whom he also obtruded them; thus paying off former crimes committed against the liberties of one people, with crimes which he urges them to commit against the lives of another.

Slave uprisings had long been a fear of the Southerners. Jefferson asserted the wrongness of the king's conquest of a "distant people who never offended him" and the miserable conditions to which they were made subject in transit, but emphasized the danger to whites. In all his subsequent conversations we can sense this same thread. He disliked slavery in theory, but despised still more the want of peace its continuation incurred. His desire that it should be ended was always qualified with the insistence the method of its end must be practicable, that is, without danger to either party.

With the wheels of revolution set in motion, Jefferson returned to Virginia, where he entered the House of Representatives. There he put forward several bills that illustrate his priorities. One was *A Bill for the More General Diffusion of Knowledge*, in which he argued that free education should be provided to the (white, male) inhabitants so that they might be well equipped to defend their rights. It began,

Whereas it appeareth that however certain

forms of government are better calculated than others to protect individuals in the free exercise of their natural rights, and are at the same time themselves better guarded against degeneracy, yet experience hath shewn, that even under the best forms, those entrusted with power have, in time, and by slow operations, perverted it into tyranny; and it is believed that the most effectual means of preventing this would be, to illuminate, as far as practicable, the minds of the people at large, and more especially to give them knowledge of those facts, which history exhibiteth, that, possessed thereby of the experience of other ages and countries, they may be enabled to know ambition under all its shapes, and prompt to exert their natural powers to defeat its purposes; [16]

Here we see illustrated Jefferson's faith in self-rule contrasted with his belief that all governments are subject to "degeneracy". Even the free nation that he hoped to emerge from the Revolutionary War chaos might lost its way and devolve into tyranny. The remedy was to prepare the people to fight against this tendency, and thus he proposed educating them in "reading, writing, and common arithmetick" as well as "Græcian, Roman, English, and American history." This last progression is by no means arbitrary. Jefferson viewed American history as the natural consequence of the Enlightenment rediscovery of Greek philosophy and Roman politics. The history of those ancient nations served as the preamble to America's own. The education bill was supplemented by *A Bill for Establishing a Public Library*. Neither was approved, but the concepts they put forward would be revisited for several years by the legislature, leading eventually to a plan for public education in 1796.

In his self-authored epitaph, Jefferson highlighted three achievements that were to him the summation of his life's worth. The first was his authorship of Declaration of Independence, the last his founding of the University of

Virginia. Between these two well-known accomplishments he included a bill put forward in 1779 and adopted into law by the State of Virginia in 1786. This was *A Bill for Establishing Religious Freedom*, or as it was called thereafter, The Virginia Statute for Religious Freedom. The document is fascinating for the glimpse it gives into Jefferson's beliefs, not only of a personal religious nature, but concerning the operation of free will. It begins, "*Well aware that the opinions and belief of men depend not on their own will, but follow involuntarily the evidence proposed to their minds*" (emphasis original). [17] Denied knowledge of alternatives, Jefferson argues, people are bound to choose the religion presented to them as truth. Asserting that "Almighty God" has ordained the exercise of free will, he argues that "attempts to influence it by temporal punishments, or burthens, or by civil incapacitations, tend only to beget habits of hypocrisy and meanness, and are a departure from the plan of the holy author of our religion". Compelling a person to belong to a religion, or punishing him for trespasses against religious tenets, produces only perfunctory public obedience, not the heartfelt observance intended by the Divine. Imposing religion by civil authority is a violation of natural right, because *"the opinions of men are not the object of civil government, nor under its jurisdiction"*. Contrary opinions must be allowed expression, for "truth is great and will prevail if left to herself ... she is the proper and sufficient antagonist to error, and has nothing to fear from the conflict unless by human interposition disarmed of her natural weapons, free argument and debate; errors ceasing to be dangerous when it is permitted freely to contradict them." Thus Jefferson neatly connects freedom of religion with freedom of speech and of the press, arguing potently for each. It is only through free expression that truth can assert herself. Such expressions are her "natural weapons", and suppressing them is an assault on her power.

Why does Jefferson personify "truth" as "her"?

The allusion is complex, having both Biblical and pagan precedents. The Book of Proverbs uses the feminine gender when personifying wisdom, for example at Proverbs 1:20-21. The Egyptian goddesses Maat and Isis, the Grecian Themis and her daughter Dike, and the Roman depiction of justice as a blindfolded woman bearing scales and a sword all correlate with Jefferson's conception. Wisdom and justice are sisters to truth, if not components of the same whole. By his adoption of this imagery, Jefferson appeals to the collective imagination. He also presents truth as a sacred entity, something to be safeguarded. In her natural state she is armed against every divisive opinion, but stripped of her weaponry, she can make no defense. "[F]ree argument", per Jefferson, must be permitted to arm her for the same reason that the colonists felt themselves entitled to take up muskets and deliver themselves from tyranny.

In the same year Jefferson was preparing his treatise on human rights, American forces won two battles of Saratoga, the Continental Congress fled Philadelphia for the second time, and George Washington's army encamped at Valley Forge. Jefferson's distance from the fighting came to an end during his time as governor of Virginia. Elected to two consecutive one-year terms by the state legislature, he was forced to flee Richmond in 1781 when Benedict Arnold's army torched the capital. Later, he watched through a spyglass as British forces invaded his own home at Monticello, having been warned by militiaman Jack Jouett just hours ahead of their arrival. The harrowing events left a deep impression on Jefferson, as did the accusations of cowardice that followed. Unlike the lionized General Washington, he preferred to fight his battles from a distance, with a quill instead of a sword.

With the end of the war came the opportunity for Jefferson to return to the national stage as delegate to the Congress of the Confederation. His most noteworthy contribution to the genesis of the country at this stage was the Land Ordinance of 1784, of which he was principle author. It provided for the apportioning of extra colonial territory into states and contained a provision banning slavery in these states after 1800. The anti-slavery ban was defeated by one vote. From this point forward, Jefferson's opinion that emancipation would have to be achieved by a later generation seems to have been set. When questioned, he wrote about its inevitability. But he no longer considered it a cause worth fighting for. His services as champion to a more broadly defined liberty were too valuable for him to squander his time on losing battles.

His sojourn in Europe while Minister to France, 1784-1789, gave him the opportunity to disseminate his views to an eager proletariat audience. He did so, of course, through their marginally aristocratic betters. Not long before his ministerial appointment, Jefferson himself had suffered through the worst period of his life.

Married in 1772 to Martha Wayles, a woman who captured his most sincere love and admiration, he became a widower in 1782. If the contemporary accounts are to be believed – and they do come from several sources – the death of Martha Jefferson nearly undid her famous husband. Fifty years after the events, eldest child Martha "Patsy" Jefferson recalled bouts of private grief from her father that were painful to witness. As had been the case after the death of his mother and sister, Jefferson made scant reference to the loss in writing. He quoted poets in the epitaphs he wrote. The master of words found his own inadequate to express his deepest feelings.

Having refused the appointment due to his wife's illness on a previous occasion, the bereaved Jefferson eagerly accepted a commission from President Washington to succeed Benjamin Franklin as Minister to France. He took along Patsy and one slave, James Hemings, whom he wished to have trained in the art of French cuisine. Like Benjamin Banneker, James Hemings was of mixed-race ancestry. His mother, Elizabeth Hemings, was said by family history to be the daughter of Susannah Epps, a pure-blooded African woman, and John Hemings, an English trader. Elizabeth, or Betty, became the property of John Wayles, who married into the Eppes family. Purportedly, Wayles took Betty as his concubine sometime after the loss of his third wife. Upon his death, Betty's children and grandchildren, numbering about 75 persons, were inherited by Thomas Jefferson through Martha, who had been the only surviving child of Wayles' first wife. This complicated legacy meant that the core of Monticello's slave labor force was populated by Jefferson's own nieces and nephews, James Hemings included. Despite his low opinion of mixed-race persons in general, Jefferson must have seen some spark in young James. Their situation in France would be very different from what it had been in Virginia.

A centerpiece of French jurisprudence was the Freedom Principle, a centuries-old notion that persons born in France were born free, and slaves entering the country were considered free the moment they passed its borders. Jefferson was well aware of this reality, and must have expected James to become aware in the fullness of time. His solution, evidently, was to enter into an agreement with the budding chef. James was to complete his training, serving Jefferson so long as he remained in his foreign assignment, then train up a replacement when the master returned home. In exchange, Jefferson granted him a monthly salary nearly double the going rate for persons in service to an affluent household, and promised to give James his freedom in America. James also had the liberty to use his free time as he wished, and to regulate his comings and goings.

One of the remarkable features of this arrangement is that evidently, James Hemings trusted his master completely. At any time during his stay in France, he might have appealed to the Admiralty Court and been granted his freedom, the legal fees being charged to the defendant in the case, Thomas Jefferson. Doubtless even the threat of such an action would have convinced Jefferson to grant a request for freedom. As a diplomat, he guarded his good name jealously. The generous terms he offered James make the most sense when viewed against the backdrop of French aristocratic society. Jefferson would at all times have been sensitive to any suggestion that his manners were delinquent. Far from aping the courtly deportment of his hosts, he strove to highlight his distinction. He set himself apart as one who was no part of the institutionalized system that oppressed the masses of France, while still being the equal of any gentleman. In Paris he mixed with artists and war heroes as well as nobles of high birth and station, all of whom inhabited a world in which one's servants were decidedly of a different class, but also genuinely obliged to their employers thanks to the sanctifying effect of commerce.

What might it have meant for Jefferson's reputation had his chattel rebelled? What would his neighbors have said? Could not the great man, the minister, the sage, the eminent democrat, conclude terms with the lowliest of his household? He lived simply (compared to the Paris elite) and dressed simply (eschewing the frippery of bows and lace that were all the rage). Could he not barter simply with his own servant? It was with a good deal of faith that Jefferson entered into a covenant with 19 year-old James, his dark-skinned, unacknowledged kinsman. How much more faith existed on James part? In the white-washed history books of the early-to-mid 20th century, Monticello was typically portrayed as a gilded cage, where happy slaves toiled in loving service to a benevolent master. While the situation was far more complicated, might there not have been a grain of truth in the myth? When Governor Jefferson fled Monticello in 1781 ahead of the British army, his slave butler

George is reported to have lied to the redcoats about the location of the family's refuge, and to have saved the silver by hiding it under a bed. George's son, the blacksmith Isaac Granger Jefferson, whose account of slave life and wartime captivity was later written up from his dictation, had nothing but fond remembrances of his "Old Master". [18] This loyalty hints that Jefferson created a tolerable work environment, at the very least.

James Hemings evidently found his master a reasonable man, when it came to business as well as philosophy. Jefferson was also a man who kept his promises. Sometime after July 15, 1787, a promise made to his late wife precipitated another promise momentous to his personal life. It was on that day that Sally Hemings, James's little sister, stepped off the boat in Paris. She had come as the nursemaid to Polly Jefferson, the youngest living daughter of Thomas and Martha. Polly and her sister Lucy had been left in the care of an aunt and uncle, but Lucy and her cousin of the same name developed whooping cough and died. From the time of her death, Jefferson determined to bring Polly to him. When the elderly nurse became ill, young Sally was chosen to accompany her mistress. In the account by Isaac Granger Jefferson, Sally is described as "mighty near white...[and] very handsome: long straight hair down her back." In the same passage, the author identifies, admittedly by hearsay, the father of Sally and her siblings. His next juxtaposition is interesting:

[Polly] & Sally went out to France a year after Mr Jefferson went. Patsy went with him at first, but she carried no maid with her. Harriet one of Sally's daughters was very handsome. Sally had a son named Madison, who learned to be a great fiddler.

It was Madison Hemings who, in 1873, brought to light the family history of a compact between Thomas Jefferson and Sally Hemings. Their story will be detailed in Chapter 7, but first let us consider its context. Having experienced life under the governance of two stepmothers herself, Martha Jefferson begged her husband not to bring a new mother into their own children's lives. Thomas swore to obey this dictum. A virile 43 year-old, he set about honoring his promise in accord with his own philosophical inclination. If he could not engage himself with women who might tempt him to matrimony, he would seek out objects for his affection with whom marriage was impossible. After all, he had experience of that sort.

Chapter 5: The Other Women

Accounts of Jefferson's grief over the loss of his wife leave little question that she was his life's great love. But their ten-year marriage was not the only time in his life when he was enthusiastically amorous. Twice in the written record, he is known to pursued another man's wife. The first occasion was when he was a young man of twenty-five. The object of his affection was Elizabeth Walker, the wife of a childhood friend. According to an account written by her husband decades after the events, Jefferson became infatuated with Elizabeth while John was on a diplomatic mission in Indian territory. Before leaving, he had entrusted his wife and baby son to Jefferson's protection, even making a will that formalized the arrangement should he not return. Years later Elizabeth confided to her husband stories of Jefferson's attempts at seduction, which she consistently repulsed. Not easily dissuaded, the future president continued his campaign even after the return of John Walker, going so far as to enter the lady's bedchamber unannounced, while her husband and his friends were dining in another room. The details of this account were published by Jefferson's political opponents, but in the wake of the scandal they inspired, he wrote a letter to Secretary of the Navy Robert Smith, confessing that in his youth he had "offered love to a handsome lady."

Mr. Jefferson's second, and more famous forbidden attraction, was to Maria Cosway. Born Maria Hadfield in 1759, the young Italian-English artist married Richard Cosway in 1770. It was an attachment that seems to have had more to do with shared interests than exclusive devotion, at least on Richard's part. Twenty years older than Maria, Richard had a reputation for eccentricity and philandering. He certainly was not jealous of his young wife's time, which Jefferson sought to monopolize after meeting the couple in Paris through a mutual friend. The freedom of pursuing a woman who did not repel his advances, in a city that did not look askance at their connection, must have been liberating for Jefferson. After the Cosways left Paris, he wrote a letter that extravagantly detailed a chiding conversation between his "Head" and his "Heart". A more telling and intimate account he never authored. It began:

Having performed the last sad office of handing you into your carriage at the Pavillon de St. Denis, and seen the wheels get actually into motion, I turned on my heel and walked, more dead than alive, to the opposite door, where my own was awaiting me. [19]

The following passage reveals his despair, and contains a remarkably candid admission.

Heart. I am indeed the most wretched of all earthly beings. Overwhelmed with grief, every fibre of my frame distended beyond its natural powers to bear, I would willingly meet whatever catastrophe should leave me no more to feel or to fear.

Head. These are the eternal consequences of your warmth and precipitation. This is one of the scrapes into which you are ever leading us. You confess your follies indeed: but still you hug and cherish them, and no reformation can be hoped, where there is no repentance.

In prosecuting its case, Jefferson's "Head" reminded his "Heart" of the extremity to which he had gone in pursuit of his amorous intentions. While Head was occupied in contemplating the architectural design of a market that might furnish the model for a new project in Richmond, Heart was "dilating with your new acquaintances, and contriving how to prevent a separation from them." The new group of friends, including the Cosways and Jefferson, all individually "had an engagement for the day. Yet all these were to be sacrificed, that you might dine together. Lying messengers were to be dispatched into every quarter of the city with apologies for your breach of engagement. You particularly had the effrontery [to] send word to the Dutchess Danville that, in the moment we were setting out to d[ine] with her, dispatches came to hand which required immediate attention. You [wanted] me to invent a more ingenious excuse; but I knew you were getting into a scrape, and I would have nothing to do with it."

Later in the letter, Jefferson attempted to plant an idea that might blossom to his great happiness. Ever eager to draw his friends close, he wrote Head's caution that the strength of his affection would only bring misery when the Cosways departed.

Heart. But they told me they would come back again the next year.

Head. But in the mean time see what you suffer: and their return too depends on so many circumstances that if you had a grain of prudence you would not count upon it. Upon the whole it is improbable and therefore you should abandon the idea of ever seeing them again.

Heart. May heaven abandon me if I do!

Head. Very well. Suppose then they come back. They are to stay here two months, and when these are expired, what is to follow? Perhaps you flatter yourself they may come to America?

Heart. God only knows what is to happen. I see nothing impossible in that supposition, and I see things wonderfully contrived sometimes to make us happy. Where could they find such objects as in America for the exercise of their enchanting art? Especially the lady, who paints landscape so inimitably. She wants only subjects worthy of immortality to render her pencil immortal. The Falling spring, the Cascade of Niagara, the Passage of the Potowmac thro the Blue mountains, the Natural bridge. It is worth a voiage across the Atlantic to see these objects; much more to paint, and make them, and thereby ourselves, known to all ages.

And our own dear Monticello, where has nature spread so rich a mantle under the eye?

The notion that Maria might follow him across the ocean is charming in its naiveté. The scrupulously religious Maria never took the suggestion seriously, even after she was parted from her unfaithful husband. Though its object was plainly to convince Mrs. Cosway of the depths of his feelings, Jefferson's Head and Heart letter has much to say about his philosophy of life in general. Ever the man of reason, he was an Epicurean in the pursuit of pleasure:

Everything in this world is matter of calculation. Advance then with caution, the balance in your hand. Put into one scale the pleasures which any object may offer; but put fairly into the other the pains which are to follow, and see which preponderates. The making an acquaintance is not a matter of indifference. When a new one is proposed to you, view it all round. Consider what advantages it presents, and to what inconveniencies it may expose you. Do not bite at the bait of pleasure till you know there is no hook beneath it. The art of life is the art of avoiding pain....

Avoiding pain, being wary of the hook in pleasure, were notions adapted by Jefferson from ancient Greek advice on life and happiness. Ruled by Head, he strove to follow them, sometimes to his detriment. Heart was more sentimental. Despite his youthful advances towards John Walker's wife, he held friendship in the highest esteem:

A friend dies or leaves us: we feel as if a limb was cut off. He is sick: we must watch over him, and participate of his pains. His fortune is shipwrecked: ours must be laid under contribution. He loses a child, a parent or a partner: we must mourn the loss as if it was our own.

The sincerity of Jefferson's friendship was a learned response to suffering. Says Heart, "This world abounds indeed with misery: to lighten its burthen we must divide it with one another." What follows is Jefferson's treatise on why Heart must rule Head in questions of a moral nature.

When the poor wearied souldier, whom we overtook at Chickahominy with his pack on his back, begged us to let him get up behind our chariot, you began to calculate that the road was full of souldiers, and that if all should be taken up our horses would fail in their journey. We drove on therefore. But soon becoming sensible you had made me do wrong, that tho we cannot relieve all the distressed we should relieve as many as we can, I turned about to take up the souldier; but he had entered a bye path, and was no more to be found: and from that moment to this I could never find him out to ask his forgiveness. Again, when the poor woman came to ask a charity in Philadelphia, you whispered that she looked like a drunkard, and that half a dollar was enough to give her for the ale-house. Those who want the dispositions to give, easily find reasons why they ought not to give. When I sought her out afterwards, and did what I should have done at first, you know that she employed the money immediately towards placing her child at school.

The accounts of the soldier and the poor woman are remarkable for their familiarity. Which of us has not been haunted by some past action or inaction, a conflict between head and heart, that a casual observer might have dismissed as unimportant? These stories highlight Jefferson's humanity, but set alongside his thoughts on black inferiority in *Notes on the State of Virginia*, they also highlight the inflexibility of his position. On how many occasions must he have observed some suffering on the part of his slaves? How often must he wondered if he was not being derelict in his duty as an emancipator of mankind in general by refusing the emancipation of his extended family in particular? These sorts of ponderings were not rightly left to Head. They rested firmly in the kingdom of Heart. Jefferson's greatest failure was that he examined them intellectually. When he contemplated slavery, he did so coldly, and self-serving intellect consistently directed him down the easy path.

On balance, Jefferson's *Head and Heart* letter is a musing on the difficulties of being governed by selfless, moral virtues. Head has its place, but it is Heart that Jefferson sees as working towards the greater good. With Head ruling unchallenged, the Revolution itself would never have happened. Says Heart,

If our country, when pressed with wrongs at the

point of the bayonet, had been governed by its heads instead of its hearts, where should we have been now? Hanging on a gallow as high as Haman's. You began to calculate and to compare wealth and numbers: we threw up a few pulsations of our warmest blood: we supplied enthusiasm against wealth and numbers: we put our existence to the hazard, when the hazard seemed against us, and we saved our country: justifying at the same time the ways of Providence, whose precept is to do always what is right, and leave the issue to him.

The personification of Providence in this passage is not particularly Jeffersonian. Though he often evoked nature as a creative force, he rarely spoke of a masculine, orchestrating God except when he knew it would endear his audience. His use of it in a letter to Maria may have been an attempt to appeal to her Catholic faith. Even in the throes of powerful emotion, in the act of pouring out his heart to a woman who had awakened feelings he had thought dead, his emotional expressions are tainted with a soupçon of calculation.

Chapter 6: The Winter Pilgrim

Autumn of 1786 was a time of upheaval for Thomas Jefferson. His passions had been excited by the presence of young Maria, perhaps for the first time since the death of his wife, and he was depressed at their parting. When the winter weather in Paris became oppressive, he departed for sunnier climes. This meant the South of France and northern Italy. It had long been his intention to make the trip, but an injury to his right wrist, presumably in some daring feat of agility that was designed to impress Mrs. Cosway, delayed him (*Head and Heart* was written left-handed). Finally, in February of 1787, on the advice of his surgeon that the wrist might benefit by being bathed in the mineral waters at Aix-en-Provence and elsewhere, he set out.

The waters did little for his wrist, which gave him trouble for the rest of his life. But the trip did ease Jefferson's mind. He indulged in two of his favorite pastimes: searching out rare books and drinking fine wine. He delighted in the weather and the classical architecture. He took the opportunity to mix with the common people, who had been excluded from the diplomatic circles of Paris, and to learn about their occupations and pastimes. "I have courted the society of gardeners, vignerons, coopers, farmers &c. and have devoted every moment of every day almost, to the business of enquiry," he wrote to the Marquis de Chastellux, a French Major General who had fought at Yorktown. Requesting an introduction to a local abbot, whom he found in the main to be obliging and pleasantly informal hosts, he asked his friend to address his return correspondence to "Monsr. Jefferson à Tours", omitting any rank or title that might have stirred up a fuss. [20]

Were Jefferson's life a novel, this pause in Jefferson's official business would serve the narrative purpose of providing breathing room between his infatuation with Maria Cosway and the beginning of the new relationship that existed in the background of the rest of his life. Jefferson returned to Paris in June of 1787. His daughter Polly arrive in July, accompanied by Sally Hemings. The baby sister of James was probably 14, but Abigail Adams, who took Polly and Sally off the ship in London before sending them across the channel, estimated 15 or 16, suggesting that she had a womanly look. Political matters seem to have absorbed Jefferson for some months after the girls' arrival, so he may not have noticed.

In America, the Constitutional Convention was in full swing. It would conclude in September, with Jefferson having commented on the drafts sent to him by multiple correspondents, among them his friend and political disciple James Madison. Of concern to Jefferson was the absence of a Bill of Rights and the lack of Presidential term limits, but he was pleased with the Constitution's general form. So high did the Declaration's author stand in the esteem of his fellow revolutionaries, and particularly his fellow Virginians, that Patrick Henry moved to reject the draft Constitution until the deficiencies that Jefferson pointed out in February of 1788 could be addressed. Ironically, by the time Henry made this motion in June of that year, Jefferson had already moved on in his opinion.

The Federalist Papers, authored by Madison, Alexander Hamilton, and John Jay, succeeded in swaying the delegates to support ratification. The complexity of the slavery issue at this time in history is richly illustrated by the inclusion of the Three-fifths Clause, originally proposed by James Madison as part of the Articles of Confederation, which mandated that, "Representatives and direct Taxes shall be apportioned among the several States which may be included within this Union, according to their respective Numbers, which shall be determined by adding to the whole Number of free Persons, including those bound to Service for a Term of Years, and excluding Indians not taxed, three fifths of all other Persons." The phrase "All other Persons", of course, referred to those in bondage without a "Term of Years". Slaves would have no direct voice in government, but their numbers would swell the influence of slave-owning states.

With the ratification crisis behind him, Jefferson turned his attention to the growing dissatisfaction of the French people in the run up to their own revolution. He hoped for a peaceful resolution of difficulties, but by whatever means change would come, he remained committed to the principles of liberty (within the appropriate spheres) for all. The Marquis de Lafayette consulted Jefferson on the content of the Declaration of the Rights of Man and of the Citizen. Jefferson's written suggestions are uncharacteristically reserved, without the flair for the dramatic evident in the Declaration of Independence. [21] Modesty and the obligations of family life seem to have warned him against rushing headlong into the debate.

But however he tried to distance himself, the mounting troubles sought him out. In July of 1789, Jefferson reported to a friend that the *Hôtel de* Langeac, his Paris home, had been robbed on three occasions. Reporting to Secretary of State John Jay, he passed on an account of mob violence:

In the afternoon a body of about 100. German cavalry were advanced and drawn up in the Place Louis XV. and about 300 Swiss posted at a little distance in their rear. This drew people to that spot, who naturally formed themselves in front of the troops, at first merely to look at them. But as their numbers increased their indignation arose: they retired a few steps, posted themselves on and behind large piles of loose stone collected in that Place for a bridge adjacent to it, and attacked the horse with stones. The horse charged, but the advantageous position of the people, and the showers of stones obliged them to retire, and even to quit the field altogether, leaving one of their number on the ground. The Swiss in their rear were observed never to stir. This was the signal for universal insurrection, and this body of cavalry, to avoid being massacred, retired towards Versailles. The people now armed themselves with such weapons as they could find in Armourer's shops and private houses, and with bludgeons, and were roaming all night through all parts of the city without any decided and practicable object. [22]

These events occurred on the 12th of July, and were a preamble to the July 14th storming of the Bastile. The outbreak of violence that followed surpassed anything that Jefferson had scene, even in the days when he had been forced to flee the British army.

Lafayette urged Jefferson to a meeting with "Members of the National Assembly – eight of us whom I want to Coalize as Being the only Means to prevent a total dissolution and a civil war." [23] Jefferson hosted the delegates and was impressed by their comportment: "The discussions began at the hour of four, and were continued till ten oclock in the evening; during which time I was a silent witness to a coolness and candor of argument unusual in the conflicts of political opinion; to a logical reasoning, and chaste eloquence, disfigured by no gaudy tinsel of rhetoric or declamation, and truly worthy of being placed in parallel with the finest dialogue of antiquity, as handed to us by Xenophon, by Plato, and Cicero." Jefferson's comparison to the great Greek orators is high praise indeed. It also emphasizes his conception of the struggle of Western civilization from enlightenment, to tyranny, and (in his day) back to enlightenment again. As modest a role as he tried to play in the proceedings, he assuredly felt justified in taking credit for having inspired the outbreak of French republicanism.

Departing himself for the Americas, Jefferson penned Mrs. Cosway a fond farewell.

I am here, my dear friend, waiting the arrival of a ship to take my flight from this side of the Atlantic and as we think last of those we love most, I profit of the latest moment to bid you a short but affectionate Adieu. ... My daughters are with me and in good health. We have left a turbulent scene, and I wish it may be tranquilized on my return, which I count will be in the month of April. Under present circumstances, aggravated as you will read them in the English papers, we cannot hope to see you in France. But a return of quiet and order may remove that bugbear, and the ensuing spring might give us a meeting at Paris with the first swallow. So be it, my dear friend, and Adieu under the hope which springs naturally out of what we wish. Once and again then farewell, remember me and love me. [24]

How bitter sweet the parting. France enchanted Jefferson, and he could not envision the turmoil that must have seemed inevitable to more objective observers.

Chapter 7: The Nature of Man

Sometime before he left Paris in 1789, Jefferson may have taken Sally Hemings as his concubine. "May have" is used here in deference to the long and hotly debated controversy lasting from 1802 into the modern day. The discreet Mr. Jefferson remained silent on the topic unto the grave, aside from the broad denial he included in the aforementioned letter to Robert Smith, in which he admitted only the Walker dalliance. Even DNA evidence has not put the question completely to rest. Many factors have served to keep the debate alive, but to a disinterested observer, the evidence in favor of a Jefferson-Hemings cohabitation was strong even before a genetic connection was shown to exist between the family lines.

Interracial paternity was common in slave-era America. Why, then, is the belief that Jefferson fathering children by a black, enslaved woman so anathema to its opponents? To some, it is because such a belief underscores the fallibility of the Founding Fathers, threatening the idea that America was a divine pronouncement, not merely a secular experiment. Others are troubled by the elevated status it gives to the African-American story in American. Still others point to the principle of American jurisprudence that pronounces a person innocent until proven guilty. Jefferson himself wrote, "I consider Trial by Jury as the only anchor yet imagined by man, by which a government can be held to the principles of its constitution." We cannot put Jefferson on trial for his conduct towards Sally Hemings. The accused is deceased, as are any witnesses. More to the point, it is not the purpose of history to condemn or to vindicate any person or persons for any foible, immoral action, or crime. The purpose of history, as Jefferson was well aware, is to pass the benefits of experience from one generation to the next.

What then can we learn from the story of Thomas Jefferson and Sally Hemings? The first and most basic lesson is that history is full of complications. No single event is so isolated and compact as it first appears. The American Revolution had its roots in ancient Greek philosophy through the person of Thomas Jefferson, among others. It also had its roots in the Atlantic slave trade and the centuries-old territorial conflicts that fueled the capture and sale of Africans by conquerors and kidnappers from rival tribes. The Unites States was never an ideal nation – the Founding Fathers never deceived themselves that it was so – it was a nation striving to apply the best lessons of history and to weave something new out of the fabric of the old. That slavery was a central and hotly debated issue from before the nation was even founded underscores this fact better than any other.

Even Benjamin Franklin, who alone challenged Jefferson's claim to being the Founding Father's brightest mind, struggled with the complexity of the issue.

Slavery is such an atrocious debasement of human nature, that its very extirpation, if not performed with solicitous care, may sometimes open a source of serious evils.

The unhappy man, who has long been treated as a brute animal, too frequently sinks beneath the common standard of the human species. The galling chains, that bind his body, do also fetter his intellectual faculties, and impair the social affections of his heart. Accustomed to move like a mere machine, by the will of a master, reflection is suspended; he has not the power of choice; and reason and conscience have but little influence over his conduct, because he is chiefly governed by the passion of fear. He is poor and friendless; perhaps worn out by extreme labor, age, and disease.

Under such circumstances, freedom may often prove a misfortune to himself, and prejudicial to society.

His lamentations are depressingly familiar, invoking the same fears that the degeneracy of the black condition would be bound to squander the benefits extended to them. But Franklin, at least, does not ascribe this degeneracy to inborn inferiority.

The way the founders dealt with the issues raised by slavery is a testimony to the fact that their vision was not pure. The tensions between George Washington and Thomas Jefferson; Thomas Jefferson and Alexander Hamilton; Thomas Jefferson and John Adams; and Jefferson and Hamilton against Aaron Burr illustrate the disunity of purpose and method with which the early champions of American independence had to contend. In the American mythological imagination, Jefferson is likened to Moses, descending from mountain with the Declaration in his hand. The mythologizers often forget that after his descent, Moses found the Israelites in open rebellion, and was able to restore order only after a divinely ordained purge. Jefferson himself would have understood the full implications of his messianic role. The banner around which all the contending statesmen (with the possible exception of Burr) could rally was the flag of Union. Having forged a nation, the greatest fear of all the founders was its dissolution.

For Jefferson, this fear rose to the level of an obsession. Combating it consumed him. He loved the nation he had helped bring to birth. Yet he did not believe it flawless. "[W]e must be contented to travel towards perfection, step by step," he wrote of the Constitution. In regarding the nation's history, it is important to regard that history as it really was, rather than as we would wish it to be. Several times in his writings Jefferson alluded to the virtues of "follow[ing] truth wherever it may lead" and not tolerating error. Certainly he would have preferred to be remembered as a flawed mortal striving to illuminate his path by the lamplight of reason, rather than be mistaken for a preening demigod devoid of human impulse.

The relationship that he was accused of entering into with Sally Hemings produced six children, four of whom lived to adulthood. In considering the possible objections to accepting Jefferson's paternity, consider that whatever the terms of their relationship, this was but one of the myriad abuses Jefferson's slaves would have been subject to on a daily basis. Born into servitude, compelled to labor at whatever task their overseers deemed appropriate, regardless of their aptitudes and preferences, and denied basic education, they gave their energies for the betterment of their masters' lot with very little hope of improving their own. The threat of violence was constant. Even the benevolent Master Jefferson walked around his demesne with whip in hand. Family life was encouraged, but breeding children was synonymous with breeding new slaves for the master to do with as he wished. Jefferson usually opted to keep families together, but it was his choice, not their own. Subservience was absolute.

Is the sexual exploitation of a 15 or 16 year-old girl out of character for a man who claimed ownership of 120 persons? How much does it tip the scale if an enslaver and profiteer from the labor of others abused one woman more? Why should we credit the testimony of those who defended Jefferson when the virtues they ascribed to him are alien to the behaviors we know to have been essential to the daily operations of his home?

Sally is at a distinct disadvantage in the narrative. She has no voice. No writings exist that relate the tale from her point of view, nor indeed give any account of her personality whatsoever. The stories we have about her are all second hand, their volume miniscule beside the mountain of Jefferson correspondence. He is a man we can come to know intimately. We can glimpse his genius and resolution, witness the greatness of his acts. All we really know of Sally is that she served in a wealthy household, in a position of trust, caring for the most sensitive member of the family; she remained in that household until the death of her master; and in the years following her mutual time with Jefferson in Paris, she bore a number of children. Nearly every other "fact" concerning her is in dispute. It is difficult to picture her, since we have no pictures of her, standing next to Jefferson. For the sake of truth, however, we should at least try.

See her now as Jefferson saw her: a young, beautiful woman, with long, straight hair trailing down her back. Full lips, dark eyes, a figure that defies concealment in her simple cotton gown. Does her forehead reach the chin of this tall, middle-aged man with his swept-back auburn hair? She has startled him coming around a corner. He steps back, stammering half an apology, then stares at her for a moment, confused. He raises his taper and shakes his head at what its light shows. It was only the darkness, his eyes seem to say, that made him mistake her for someone else. She is only his servant, his daughter's nurse. She has spent too long in the house, a refugee from the damp and cold of winter. Her skin will darken when the sun returns. A month of summer and he will no longer see the blush of her cheeks as she nods and curtseys and averts her eyes, as now she does. She turns, with a swish of skirt, and in two strides is at her door. She will turn the handle, pass the threshold, be gone until the morrow.

She will turn the handle and be gone. Unless he bids her, "Wait."

Chapter 8: Duty and Domesticity

Of all Jefferson's virtues, his capacity for forming deeply emotive friendships is the most endearing. "I find friendship to be like wine, raw when new, ripened with age, the true old man's milk and restorative cordial," he once wrote. His attachment to Dabney Carr, school chum and brother-in-law, his grief at the loss of sister Jane, and the evident affection in his letters to John and Abigail Adams, show him to be a man of empathy and fellow feeling. John Adams is an interesting case, as political differences eventually drove a wedge between the two men, even as Jefferson served under Adams as his Vice President. When their turn in the spotlight was finished, the two resumed their regular friendly correspondence. There will be more to say about their exchanges in due course. In the meantime, consider another close friend, one who stayed the course, united politically and personally with Jefferson through their mutual public service and beyond. That man was James

Madison.

The future fourth president and Father of the Constitution was a Virginia planter, like Jefferson. Also like Jefferson, he credited a Scotsman – in his case, the private tutor Donald Robertson – with molding his worldview. He missed sharing an alma mater with Jefferson due to his sensitive health (George Washington and Jefferson both commented on the unhealthful effects of mosquito breeding tidewater at Williamsburg, the home of William and Mary College), but obtained a respectable education at the College of New Jersey, located in and later re-named in honor of Princeton. Like Jefferson, Madison was not an orthodox Christian, holding personal or perhaps deist beliefs. Their physical dissimilarity was striking. At 6'2", Jefferson stood nose-to-nose with George Washington as America's tallest president, before the coming of the man in the stove pipe hat. Madison was and remains, at the time of writing, our shortest Chief Executive, at 5'4".

It was during Madison's service in the Virginia legislature in 1776 that he came to the attention of Jefferson. When Jefferson became Governor in 1779, Madison served on his counsel, and the two developed a habit of regular conversation that would carry over into a written correspondence during Jefferson's time in France. Madison had an almost unique talent for moderating his philosophical friend's excesses, divining the sober course that might make the best use of Jefferson's radical ideas. When Jefferson, from Paris, made a seminal suggestion that national laws should be subject to term limits, expiring every 19 years, Madison suggested that the present society was not ready for a course correction so visionary and sublime.

Another of Madison's gift was his ability to rouse Jefferson to action. After returning to Monticello in late 1789, Jefferson was offered the position of Secretary of State under President Washington, but he demurred. Thanking the president for the offer, he wrote his concerns about the duties of the post:

Could any circumstance seduce me to overlook the disproportion between its duties and my talents it would be the encouragement of your choice. But when I contemplate the extent of that office, embracing as it does the principal mass of domestic administration, together with the foreign, I cannot be insensible of my inequality to it: and I should enter on it with gloomy forebodings from the criticisms and censures of a public just indeed in their intentions, but sometimes misinformed and misled, and always too respectable to be neglected. I cannot but foresee the possibility that this may end disagreeably for one, who, having no motive to public service but the public satisfaction, would certainly retire the moment that satisfaction should appear to languish. [25]

The idea that as the Secretary of State, he would be taking on significant domestic responsibilities was a misunderstanding on Jefferson's part, but it also reflects his desire to involve himself in the evolution of American governance. He seems to have been aware of this urge within himself. His absence from the Constitutional Convention galled him, despite having so excellent a mouthpiece as Madison to voice his ideas. Madison, was, after all, his own man. Though the two men agreed on nearly every political principle, there were differences in emphasis that Jefferson would have sensed more keenly than anyone else. He was not a man content to have others speak for him, and the liberty for which he campaigned was personal as well as national. Competing with his eagerness to involve himself in democratic politics was his aversion to criticism, largely stemming from accusations of cowardice and mismanagement that dogged him after the abandonment of Richmond during the Revolutionary War. His initial reaction to this criticism had been to withdraw, as soon as he was able, from public life, and he accepted his post as a foreign ambassador partially because it insulated him from critics, while still allowing him to mix in influential circles. In this respect, his partnership with Madison was the best of both worlds – political influence layered with anonymity. He could withdraw with his family, with his books, and with his mistress in peace, while still wielding influence in the democracy that was, it must be allowed, an ideal he cherished more in the abstract than the particular.

Returning to France was preferable, and he argued to President Washington the advantage of familiarity. "The ground I have already passed over enables me to see my way into that which is before me," he wrote. Though the situation in France was increasingly perilous, part of him longed to bear personal witness to its outworking. "The change of government, too, taking place in the country where it is exercised, seems to open a possibility of procuring from the new rulers some new advantages in commerce which may be agreeable to our countrymen."

The altruistic motive he ascribes to himself here is not genuine; having lighted the lamp of freedom, he wanted to watch it burn. However, as he wrote Washington, "it is not for an individual to choose his post." Only if Washington were himself indifferent to which posting Jefferson should choose, as Secretary of State or Minister to Paris, would Jefferson insert his own judgment in the place of the president's. Alternately apprehensive and ambitious, Jefferson was loyal to the duly constituted authority of the president.

At Washington's direction, Madison clarified the responsibilities of the new position to his mentor. Jefferson was not to concern himself substantially with domestic policy, but advise on foreign affairs, the whole nation benefiting from those experiences that enabled him to "see [his] way". Yielding to Madison's flattery and persuasion, Jefferson accepted Washington's request. In March of 1790 he began his term of service as first Secretary of State.

The seat of government to which Jefferson transferred was in New York City. In making the move, he left behind his acknowledged family, chief among them the newly married Patsy, and his unacknowledged family, the Hemingses, including Sally.

According to Madison Hemings, the first of his siblings was born soon after his mother's return to Monticello, but died soon after. James Callendar's 1802 exposé contradicts this account, pointing to Thomas Woodson as Jefferson's surviving eldest son, but DNA evidence evaluated in 1998 conclusively disproved this connection. It therefore appears that Jefferson left a newly bereaved young mother at Monticello. He knew well the pain of loss, particularly the loss of a child. Whatever comfort he may have offered, whether personally or through an agent, is unrecorded.

Chapter 9: A Divided House

The relationship between Washington and Jefferson began on cordial grounds. Both men had been members of the Virginia House of Burgesses, Washington from 1755 and Jefferson from 1769, until the dissolution of that institution in 1775. They had conspired together with their fellow Burgesses and fought for the new nation in the Revolution – Washington with his sword and Jefferson with his quill – and their early letters reflect mutual admiration, if little warmth. Though Washington was considerably younger than Peter Jefferson would have been had he lived, and older than the Jefferson patriarch was when he died, the similarity in the two men's backgrounds could not have escaped Thomas Jefferson's notice, nor failed to magnify his esteem. Their schism came about due to Jefferson's growing rivalry with Alexander Hamilton, Washington's Secretary of the Treasury.

In retrospect, the two men seem natural opponents. Though both had improved their economic status through advantageous marriages, what fortune Jefferson began with was inherited, while Hamilton's was self-made. The Jefferson and Wayles names were well-known among the Virginia elite. Hamilton was a bastard, and foreign born, which closed to him the prospect of obtaining the nation's highest office. While Jefferson had spent the Revolutionary War caring for his gubernatorial duties, or in hiding, Hamilton distinguished himself on the battlefield alongside General Washington. Both men were known for eloquence and the forthrightness of their beliefs, but Hamilton was an orator, while Jefferson shrank from public speaking. The biggest difference that became evident in the four years of President Washington's first administration was that Jefferson was a dreamer, an idealist, while Hamilton sought practical solutions to emergent problems. During Jefferson's own presidential administration he would prove himself an able compromiser, but this pragmatism was not evident to those who became his political foes.

These foes eventually coalesced as the Federalist Party, who counted Vice President John Adams among their members. Sensitive to the perils of the separate States' war time debt, both to sovereign powers and former militia, Hamilton and the Federalists advocated for the assumption of that debt by the federal government. To collect revenue and repay the debt required the further creation of a national bank. When the assumption question was brought up to a vote in the House, it failed by only three votes. Unpopular with states who had already made inroads into their own debt repayment, opposing congressmen led by James Madison, also asserted that assumption would reward wealthy speculators from Northern states who had been buying up continental currency and scrip held by war veterans. These speculators offered bargain-basement prices for the greatly depreciated currencies, in the belief that the government would eventually make good on demands to redeem it at face value. Ultimately, this was exactly what occurred. In an early example of his political agility, it was Jefferson who helped Hamilton to broker the deal.

"Going to the President's one day I met Hamilton as I approached the door. His look was sombre, haggard, and dejected beyond description. Even his dress uncouth and neglected. He asked to speak with me. We stood in the street near the door. He opened the subject of the assumption of the state debts, the necessity of it in the general fiscal arrangement and its indispensible necessity towards a preservation of the union," wrote Jefferson. [26] The appeal to "preservation of the union," touched on the common interest of both men and certainly strengthened Hamilton's appeal to his future rival. As he had done in France for Lafayette, Jefferson agreed to host a summit between Hamilton and his contending protégé. The result of their cordial dinner meeting was the Compromise of 1790, in which the assumption was established by law. In exchange, Hamilton agreed to support Madison's plan to locate the national capitol on the Potomac, rather than pushing for its location in a financial center, such as his home state of New York. Recounting the events of the dinner, Jefferson claimed only have brought the parties together, not to have influenced the outcome, but his hospitality was surely an inspiration to Madison.

Whatever sympathy Jefferson had towards Hamilton dissolved when Hamilton issued his proposal for operating the new bank. Jefferson objected on several points, enumerating these to President Washington in a private letter. Among his concerns were Hamilton's modification to concepts of land holding (mortmain) and inheritance. Jefferson felt that the national government had no legal basis for imposing its own definition of these concepts on the states. His argument hinged on one of the central tenets of his personal political beliefs, the strict constructionist view of the Constitution. He expounded on this perspective in a formal statement requested by Washington, his *Opinion on the Constitutionality of the Bill for Establishing a National Bank*. "I consider the foundation of the Constitution as laid on this ground that 'all powers not delegated to the U.S. by the Constitution, not prohibited by it to the states, are reserved to the states or to the people'," he stated, citing the Tenth Amendment. "To take a single step beyond the boundaries thus specially drawn around the powers of Congress, is to take possession of a boundless field of power, no longer susceptible of any definition." [27] That the founding of banks was not a power expressly granted to the legislature by the Constitution, according to Jefferson, should be interpreted as a strict prohibition against it. Jefferson enumerated the financial powers granted to the U. S. by that document, none of which would expressly support the creation of such an institution.

He then went on to discuss the implied powers of the government. The conservatism of his position is underscored by his commentary on "general phrases" conveying those powers.

The second general phrase is 'to make all laws necessary and proper for carrying into execution the enumerated powers.' But they can all be carried into execution without a bank. A bank therefore is not necessary, and consequently not authorised by this phrase.

It has been much urged that a bank will give great facility, or convenience in the collection of taxes. Suppose this were true: yet the constitution allows only the means which are 'necessary' not those which are merely 'convenient' for effecting the enumerated powers. If such a latitude of construction be allowed to this phrase as to give any non— enumerated power, it will go to every one, for these is no one which ingenuity may not torture into a convenience, in some way or other, to some one of so long a list of enumerated powers. It would swallow up all the delegated powers, and reduce the whole to one phrase as before observed. Therefore it was that the constitution restrained them to the necessary means, that is to say, to those means without which the grant of the power would be nugatory.

Jefferson's fear was that opening the door to the national bank would start a rapid deterioration of the protections offered by the Constitution against tyrannical powers. The use of any power that had not been spelled out as belonging to the government would invite abuse. Rule by the few could be just as dictatorial as rule by the one, as the colonies' troubles with Parliament showed. The system of checks and balances devised by the Convention, and promoted by Madison's *Federalist Papers* was not then a functioning entity. The chief executive's powers were miniscule, and the Supreme Court under John Jay had yet to hear its first case. Jefferson had seen enough of President Washington to believe him sincerely uninterested in amassing personal power. This modesty was absolutely essential to the health of the new union, but it left Congress as the one domestic threat to individual autonomy.

A conflict existed between Jefferson's idealism and the financial realities of the day. In its fledgling state, America was essentially two nations, one of back-country farmers, such as Jefferson himself, and another of merchants and manufacturers (there was a third nation of slaves, but these went unconsidered). To Jefferson's mind, the livelihood and freedom of the farmers – who predominated in the South – depended on the America developing into an agrarian society. He envisioned an America whose citizens were largely self-sufficient. Manufacturing would be left to the Old World nations, who would barter for America's primary goods. The government would be financed through tariffs on imports, which tariffs would also serve to limit industrialization. There would be little need for the government to involve itself in citizens' day-to-day lives. Land-owning white Americans could be free to live as they pleased, surrounded by like-minded individualists. The one major omission in this idealistic vision was a standing military capable of resisting invasion. But Jefferson's generation had seen the military potential of an amateur force united in common cause. They had prevailed against the greatest power in the world, largely through determination and geographic isolation. Jefferson saw Britain as a fading power, and France as a soon-to-be sister nation, united in liberty. Though the European nations still represented a threat to the unconquered West, he was justified in thinking that the Old World would not have the resources to conduct a war of conquest for decades to come.

In his "Final Version of an Opinion on the Constitutionality of an Act to Establish a Bank", Hamilton laid out his contrary opinion.

[T]his general principle is inherent in the very definition of Government and essential to every step of the progress to be made by that of the United States; namely—that every power vested in a Government is in its nature sovereign, and includes by force of the term, a right to employ all the means requisite, and fairly applicable to the attainment of the ends of such power; and which are not precluded by restrictions & exceptions specified in the constitution; or not immoral, or not contrary to the essential ends of political society. [28]

In saying that power is vested in Government unless where precluded, Hamilton was reversing Jefferson's argument entirely. He added that it would be incumbent on opponents to show "that a rule which in the general system of things is essential to the preservation of the social order is inapplicable to the United States." The burden of proof rested with the resisters of sovereign power, with those who sought to restrict strong national rule, not those who wished to invoke it. Implied powers, says Hamilton, have the same force of law as express powers. He also introduces the concept of resulting powers, that is, powers that devolve from the use of powers either express or implied. Conquest of a neighboring territory – a power expressly granted the U. S. government – necessitates the power to impose rule. By these arguments, Hamilton sought to show that the formation of the National Bank and its operation by a funded corporation created for the purpose was a right of government. In Hamilton's loose constructionist view, government was to operate with a presumption of right, taking whatever steps it deemed appropriate. To Hamilton, the checks and balances of the three party system were sufficient to any regulatory task.

Hamilton's arguments prevailed, and the National Bank was founded. President Washington was by no means wholehearted in his support, going so far as to draft a veto of the bank bill. Like Jefferson, he feared the encroachments of government on Americans' daily lives. But Washington was a pragmatist. Duty for him was a clarion call. If a perfect solution to the problems of debt repayment, particularly where it touched his own soldiers, could not be found, he preferred the imperfect solution to no solution at all. In this readiness to take action, he differed from Secretary of State Jefferson, who clung to dreams of an ideal agrarian republic.

At its core, the Jefferson-Hamilton debate concerned the nature of power. Do the people need protection from the abuse of power by their elected representatives or the imposition of power by external actors? Clearly, both protections are necessary. Where Jefferson and Hamilton disagreed was in which would be the gravest and more persistent danger.

Chapter 10: A War of Words

Not content to argue their case before the president, both Hamilton and Jefferson took their feud to the press. Hamilton went first, creating the *Gazette of the United States* in 1789. Under various pseudonyms, he and John Adams among others espoused their belief in the necessity of strong central government. In response, Jefferson and Madison tapped Madison's college friend, the poet Phillip Freneau, to edit the *National Gazette* in 1792. Unapologetically partisan, both papers lampooned the head men of their opposite parties, representing them as extremists determined to scuttle the ship of State. Jefferson and Madison, per the G. of the U. S., were hopeless dreamers and closeted aristocrats, whose paranoid delusions and selfish economic views blinded them to the national interest. According to the National Gazette, Hamilton and Adams were rabid monarchists, abusing their privileged positions to amass fortunes for themselves and their money changer friends.

To Jefferson, a man who treasured the good opinion of his friends, the rivalry with Adams must have been a bitter pill. As Vice President, Adams had the ear of his chief, all the more so because Washington was a subscriber to his *Gazette*. Adams' writings were as esoteric as Jefferson's own. Published in the *Gazette of the United States* in 1790, his *Discourses on Davila, a series of papers, on political history* was a favorite target of the opposing press. Voluminous and far-reaching, the *Discourses* outlined Adam's political philosophy under the guise of translating the *Historia delle guerre civili di Francia by Enrico Caterino Davila from the original Italian. Adams passed gradually from translating the work concerning the sixteenth-century French civil wars to likening the events of Davila's history to contemporary times. Using this device he commented on the contemporary French troubles and drew likenesses to America's own genesis. Critiquing the French system, Adams argued that laws could not ultimately be made without distinction between small and great, rich and poor. The French claimed to eliminate all such distinctions, but Adams in Divala contended that this was as impossible as it was to make "all men and women equally wise, elegant and beautiful". [29]*

Freneau's Gazette attacked Divala as an attempt at dazzling the public with vain historical allusions. In his "Rules for Changing a Limited Republican Government into an Unlimited Hereditary One" he wrote a 15-point list satirizing Adams' point of view. Rule 5 advised that the anti-Republican press should "be busy in propagating the doctrines of monarchy and aristocracy". A useful method for doing so was to "confound a mobbish democracy with a representative republic". *Divala* had portrayed the new French government as just such a mob. Freneau coyly advised:

Review all the civil contests, convulsions, factions, broils, squabbles, bickering, black eyes, and bloody noses of ancient, middle, and modern ages; caricature them into the most frightful forms and colors that can be imagined, and unfold one scene of horrible tragedy after another till the people be made, if possible, to tremble at their own shadows. Let the discourses on Davila then contrast with these pictures of terror the quiet hereditary succession, the reverence claimed by birth and nobility, and the fascinating influence of stars, and ribands, and garters, cautiously suppressing all the bloody tragedies and unceasing oppressions which form the history of this species of government. [30]

Here Freneau charges that Adam's perception of history was flawed. It elevated the "ribands, and garters" – the honorary and decorative trappings of aristocracy – and asserted that hereditary successions, in contrast to revolution, were peaceful affairs. This was in blatant disregard for the "bloody tragedies and unceasing oppressions" that monarchical forms of government routinely imposed. Though grandly overblown, Freneau's words were in line with public sympathies of the time. Americans were wary of monarchical ambitions. Merchants and farmers alike wanted to chart their own course, not kowtow to an invincible legislature.

Partisan as it was, Freneau's article miscontrued Adams' treatise, which celebrated the essential quality of balance between the branches of government. "The great art of law-giving," wrote Adams, "consists in balancing the poor against the rich in the legislature, and in constituting the legislative a perfect balance against the executive power, at the same time that no individual or party can become its rival." His advocacy of enlarged executive powers was in response to their relative weakness. Despite the reasonableness of this argument, the unpopular position cost Adams much in the way of political currency. On the title page of his personal copy of the collected Davila essays, published in 1805, Adams wrote the following marginal note:

This dull, heavy volume still excites the wonder of its author. First that he could find, amidst the constant scenes of business and dissipation in which he was enveloped, time to write it. Secondly that he had the courage to oppose and publish his own opinions to the universal opinion of all America, and indeed of almost all mankind. Not one man in America then believed him. He know not one then, and has not heard of one since, who then believed him. The work, however, powerfully operated to destroy his popularity. It was urged as full proof that he was an advocate for monarchy and labouring to introduce a hereditary President and Senate in America. [31]

"Not one man in America" was certainly hyperbolic, but in the aftermath of his political drubbing by Jefferson in the election of 1801, it must have seemed to Adams that he had not a friend in the world. Adams, however, was not a man who needed friends to stabilize his ambition. In contrast, Jefferson's ambition waxed and waned from day to day.

Describing the conflict between Jefferson and Hamilton, President Washington wrote one of his most memorable turns of phrase. "How unfortunate, and how much is it to be regretted then, that whilst we are encompassed on all sides with avowed enemies and insidious friends, that internal dissensions should be harrowing and tearing our vitals." [32] This verbal and textual evisceration had all the trappings of political theater, including a sex scandal. From early 1791 until sometime in 1792, Alexander Hamilton had conducted an affair with a married woman, Maria Reynolds, whose husband, James, blackmailed the Secretary in return for his silence and continued access to his wife. More than $1000 changed hands before Mr. Reynolds was caught in a scheme involving the back-pay of Revolutionary War soldiers, a scenario similar to that which had motivated James Madison to oppose national assumption of war debt. When Hamilton refused to help Reynolds further, the blackmailer revealed the affair to Hamilton's enemies, naturally minimizing his own iniquitous behavior. The affair was hushed up after an investigation headed by James Monroe – Madison's later Secretary of State and War, and another Jeffersonian disciple – for the sake of the nation, but copies of incriminating letters were set aside for a later day.

While his nemesis attended to personal affairs, Jefferson was concerned about the news from France. Bloodier and more tragic than he had ever envisioned, the French Revolution had by 1792 taken on an apocalyptic air, ahead of still more murderous days to come. Jefferson was hard pressed to defend the actions of the revolutionaries with whom he had felt so much common cause. By January of 1793, the writing was on the wall: the American experiment had yielded bitter fruit in France. Still Jefferson was unwilling to withdraw his support. He saw the French excesses as part of the price to be paid for the deliverance from superstition, oppression, and the domination of the many by the few. He wrote to still another p*rotégé,* diplomat William Short,

In the struggle which was necessary, many guilty persons fell without the forms of trial, and with them some innocent. These I deplore as much as anybody, and shall deplore some of them to the day of my death. But I deplore them as I should have done had they fallen in battle. ... [T]ime and truth will rescue and embalm their memories, while their posterity will be enjoying that very liberty for which they would never have hesitated to offer up their lives. The liberty of the whole earth was depending on the issue of the contest, and was ever such a prize won with so little innocent blood? My own affections have been deeply wounded by some of the martyrs to this cause, but rather than it should have failed, I would have seen half the earth desolated. Were there but an Adam and an Eve left in every country, and left free, it would be better than as it now is. I have expressed to you my sentiments, because they are really those of 99 in an hundred of our citizens. [33]

The passage is exaggerated in its expression, but genuine in its sentiment. For Jefferson, no sacrifice was too great for the noble cause of ending tyranny...provided that the tyrant in question was not himself.

The contrast between Jefferson's stated ideal and the realities of the world in which he lived can be illustrated by a strange event involving his extended family. Dubbed the Bizarre Scandal, owing to the plantation of its principle actors holding that name, the drama centered around the eighteen year-old Ann Cary Randolph, a sister-in-law to Patsy Jefferson. Unmarried and under the care of her brother-in-law, Richard Randolph, Ann was believed by her relatives to be pregnant, months after the death of her suitor. Theodorick Randolph, Richard's brother, had courted Ann, but developed consumption and died in February 1792. Ann's condition was noted over the summer, and on October 1st, she was confined to her bed with an unspecified illness that lasted a week. This confinement had taken place during a family visit to friend. Afterward, some slaves of the Randolph's host claimed to have discovered the body of an infant hidden in the woodpile. The account spread by whispers and innuendo. Conflicting theories were discussed at fashionable Virginia gatherings. Had young Ann and her lover yielded to temptation in the last days before his death? Had Richard, in comforting her, seduced the girl? Had the baby been stillborn? Or had Richard destroyed the infant, to protect his reputation or his brother's memory, or in a rage at her condition?

Richard was arrested, or himself brought a charge of slander to court – accounts differ as to which. Whatever the case, the trial that ensued involved some of the most celebrated legal minds of the age, including John Marshall and Patrick Henry, both of whom were engaged by the Randolphs. Nothing could be proved, no child's corpse having been brought forward, but Richard Randolph never quite managed to outrun the rumors of his culpability. He died three years later, withered by distress. His wife, in the meantime, developed a dislike of sister Ann, and made her life rather miserable thereafter. Reading of the furor in the Virginia papers, Jefferson counseled Patsy to extend Ann every kindness. "For her it is the moment of trying the affection of her friends, when their commiseration and comfort become balm to her wounds. I hope you will deal them out to her in full measure, regardless of what the trifling or malignant may think or say." [34] It was an enlightened man's view of the situation, merciful and compassionate. In his imagination he conceived a world where self-sufficient Americans were capable of governing themselves serenely, doing no harm. He was not about to condemn a bereaved young woman for indiscretions that were, at worst, a folly of youth. His own follies had not all had access even to that excuse.

Chapter 11: The Farmer's Son

Ever the man of the hour, President Washington agreed to return to office for a second term once his first came to its end. Whether the storms that had plagued their relationship for the past three years had shown signs of passing, or merely for the sake of the country, Washington entreated Jefferson to stay on as Secretary of State. Madison, too, urged his commander to remain, appealing to Jefferson's distaste for the bad opinion of *hoi polloi*. Jefferson declined. "To my fellow-citizens the debt of service has been fully and faithfully paid," he told Madison. Acknowledging that a duty had been owed, he asserted that its term could not be indefinite, "for that would be to be born a slave." This is the Aristotelian philosophy, wherein some are born in a natural state of slavery, lacking certain qualities of the soul. Jefferson asserts that he is a whole man, and thus subject to a limited term of service to the public good. Service to his own friends was another matter, but in this respect also, Jefferson had given all that was owing. His friends were free agents, and could stand on their merits, no longer needing his reputation to prop up their own.

If the public then has no claim on me, and my friends nothing to justify, the decision will rest on my own feelings alone. There has been a time when these were very different from what they are now: when perhaps the esteem of the world was of higher value in my eye than everything in it. But age, experience, and reflection, preserving to that only it's due value, have set a higher on tranquility. The motion of my blood no longer keeps time with the tumult of the world. It leads me to seek for happiness in the lap and love of my family, in the society of my neighbors and my books, in the wholesome occupations of my farm and my affairs, in an interest or affection in every bud that opens, in every breath that blows around me, in an entire freedom of rest or motion, of thought or incogitancy, owing account to myself alone of my hours and actions. [35]

Personal feeling had once inclined him against an early retirement. Now they moved him now to take shelter from the political hubbub. He wanted no more to do with the "tumult of the world" – Federalists and Anti-Federalists, monarchists and republicans, Hamilton's bank and the anarchic blood spilling of the French dissolution – but a peaceful life at home. In his fifth decade of life, he wanted for himself what he had worked to secure for others. He wanted freedom.

Had he set aside his fears for the nation and its great experiment in liberty? No indeed. But he did despair of doing his country further good.

Worn down with labours from morning till night, and day to day; knowing them as fruitless to others as they are vexatious to myself, committed singly in desperate and eternal contest against a host who are systematically undermining the public liberty and prosperity, even the rare hours of relaxation sacrificed to the society of persons in the same intentions, of whose hatred I am conscious even in those moments of conviviality when the heart wishes most to open itself to the effusions of friendship and confidence, cut off from my family and friends, my affairs abandoned to chaos and derangement, in short giving every thing I love, in exchange for everything I hate, and all this without a single gratification in possession or prospect, in present enjoyment or future wish.

In short, he was tired. Frustration over his defeats at Hamilton's hands and the unpleasant taste of partisanship combined to sour him on his high position. He longed for farm, home, and family. And so he resigned. President Washington was generous, heaping praise on his former secretary, assuring Jefferson that his contributions had been valued. His words were kind, though probably insincere.

In January of 1794, Jefferson returned to live full-time at Monticello. He busied himself in every form of agrarian activity, bringing a number of innovations to the plantation, including the nailery where he employed boys from 10-16 years of age. He rose at dawn and started each day by soaking his feet in cold water. He dressed comfortably if somewhat eclectically and stuffed his pockets with a compass, thermometer, and drawing implements. Never absent his person was the small ivory notebook in which he jotted down measurements and observations, later to be copied into the permanent records.

Monticello changed its face and shape throughout Jefferson's life, but its major renovation started at this time. True to his vision for a self-sufficient America, Jefferson added numerous shops for the manufacture of finished goods. While the workmen labored, Jefferson rode his horses, fished, and hunted.

He played with his grandchildren Anne, Thomas, and Ellen. And, it seems, he carried on in his arrangement with Sally Hemings. In 1795 Hemings gave birth to her second child, a daughter named Harriet. According to family history, Jefferson was the father.

Throughout his attempted retirement, Jefferson made a gradual return to his political mindset. He claimed to have quit reading newspapers in February 1794, but kept in close contact with James Madison, advising him on general political matters as well as the rapidly consolidating power of the new Republican party. Among the most consequential events of this period was a mission to London undertaken by John Jay. The treaty that Jay concluded was heavily influenced by Hamilton, who wished to strengthen trade relations with Great Britain. In exchange, Britain agreed to withdraw from pre-revolutionary forts in the Northwest Territory and permit some limited trade with their Caribbean and Indian possessions. To

Jeffersonians, the treaty utterly failed to address several driving issues of the day went largely unresolved in John Jay's Treaty. There was no settlement of Revolutionary War debt. Worse, the seizure of American vessels that Britain suspected of doing business with its enemy France, was winked at, the treaty conceding that Britain had the right to search ships for French goods, though being liable only to pay recompense to ship owners. These concessions were seen as infringing on America's sovereignty, and public dissatisfaction with the treaty turned it into a black eye for Washington's administration. Years later, during John Adams' presidency, the anti-French provisions of the treaty would ignite a naval cold war. [36]

By April of 1795, Madison thought Jefferson had rested long enough. His letters urged his chief to take steps towards succeeding Washington as president. At first Jefferson refused. He had not yet grown weary of Monticello's charms, and contented himself with entertaining prominent

Republican figures in his home. One such figure was Senator Aaron Burr of New York, whose star was on the rise thanks to his leading role in opposing Jay's Treaty.

Never truly absent from the halls of power, Jefferson's patience for life behind the scenes wore thin as the hour for President Washington's departure approached. Jefferson's enemies in the Federalist party regarded him as the candidate to fear, and stories of Governor Jefferson fleeing Richmond during the Revolution were published in Federalist papers, portraying him as a coward, unworthy of the nation's confidence. Having reneged on his pledged to avoid newspapers, these reports goaded Jefferson. The Republican press responded that the Federalist's picked candidate, Vice President Adams, was a monarchist who would wreck the American experiment in liberty by installing legislators and himself in office for life. That he would stand for the presidency was a belief Jefferson allowed to grow rather than actively fostered. He did not campaign for the office, and only assured supporters that he would do as honor directed. Imitating Washington in modesty was certainly a sound political strategy at a time when the central issue of partisan politics was how much power should be invested in a single man, and for how long.

The contest was brutish and indelicate. On October 19, 1796, the attacks became extremely personal when Hamilton's *Gazette of the United States* accused Jefferson of carrying on a sexual relationship with a slave. A political cartoon depicted Jefferson's head on a rooster's body, accompanied by a dark-complexioned hen. The caption read, "A PHILOSOPHIC COCK". Having fallen out with Adams sometime before, Hamilton favored neither of the contenders for president and offered his own candidate, Thomas Pinckney, as an alternative. Federalists accepted the South Carolinian Pinckney in the hopes that they could induce southern voters to support the Yankee Adams, with Pinckney as his

Vice President. As specified in the Constitution, the Vice Presidency was to go to the second-place winner of the election. Hamilton hoped that Federalist candidates could thus claim both top spots in the Executive. With careful management, he might even be able to manuever the malleable Pinckney into the top spot. Jefferson's Republican allies nominated Aaron Burr as their Vice Presidential candidate, again balancing Southern and Northern interests.

When the ballots were counted, Adams placed first with 71 electoral votes. Jefferson trailed by only three votes, at 68, with Pinckney a distant third. Gracious in defeat, Vice President-elect Jefferson drafted a congratulatory letter to Adams. He sent it first to James Madison to get his friend's opinion, and Madison convinced him not to send it, on the ground that Jefferson might be embarrassed should the letter later be produced as evidence of sympathy for the opposition. Partisan politics were the new reality, and party loyalty trumped the sacred bond of friendship. The years of Jefferson's Vice Presidency would be among the most divisive and contentious of his political career.

Chapter 12: Crimes and Punishments

President Adams' administration was one long trudge from disaster to disaster, varying only in its alteration from foreign to domestic troubles and back again. Jay's Treaty having squandered the good will of France, Americans lived in fear of French reprisal. A proclamation of the Revolutionary government in 1796 allowed French ships to seize American merchant vessels. In response, President Adams sent envoys to negotiate a peace with their former ally. Refused an audience with Foreign Minister Talleyrand, the envoys met instead with four of his representatives, identified in state papers as W, X, Y, and Z. Through these intermediaries, Talleyrand demanded bribes for his country and for himself. The appalled Americans refused. Pushing for capitulation, the negotiators threatened war, and Talleyrand, finally putting in an appearance, denied requests to stop seizing American vessels. Adams put America on a war footing. In so doing, he made the great blunder of his presidency.

"Be it enacted by the Senate and the House of Representatives of the United States of America in Congress assembled, That it shall be lawful for the President of the United States at any time during the continuance of this act, to order all such aliens as he shall judge dangerous to the peace and safety of the United States, or shall have reasonable grounds to suspect are concerned in any treasonable or secret machinations against the government thereof, to depart out of the territory of the United States," began *An Act Concerning Aliens*. This new Act was one of four passed by the House and Senate in November 1797 and signed into law the next July. Its companion, *An Act for the Punishment of Certain Crimes Against the United States* criminalized slander and libel against the "government of the United States, or either house of the Congress of the United States, or the President of the United States, with intent to defame". [39] To the Republicans, this was tantamount to crowning Adams and his supporters as petty kings, defended from censure by force of law. Jefferson himself suggested that the Acts were a test of how far the American public would permit its officers to stretch their Constitutional powers, preparatory to the establishment of hereditary monarchy.

Protests for and against the Alien and Sedition Acts resulted in violence, combatants wearing British black or French red, white and blue cockades – circular clusters of ribbons – pinned to their hats. [40] The symbolism is striking. In its twenty-second year, citizens of the United States still felt the need to identify themselves by the attitudes and sympathies of nations of the Old World. The stigma of appearing to support one of two past and potential enemies of the country was not enough motivation for Americans to overcome their crisis of identity. This might have seemed a grim presentiment of eventual dissolution to observers of the time,

Jefferson included. However, there was a silver lining for Republicans. The very act of assembling in organized protest was, after all, a republican act, evoking the spirit of '76.

The really shocking thing about the Acts of Sedition was that they were actually enforced. Benjamin Franklin Bache, who had exposed the "XYZ Affair" (wither W?) was arrested while the Acts were still under discussion. Released on $4000 bail, Bache died of yellow fever before his trial. [41] Congressman Matthew Lyon of Vermont, a veteran Green Mountain Boy was accused of libeling the president in a published letter. Convicted to four months imprisonment and a fine of $1000, Lyons campaigned for reelection from prison and was returned to the House of Representatives by his Northern constituency. [42] Of special significance to Jefferson was the arrest of James Thomson Callender. In 1797, Callender had published a pamphlet exposing Alexander Hamilton's affair with Mrs. Reynolds in 1797. The source of

Callender's information was evidently James Monroe, since the pamphlet reprinted letters Monroe had copied during the investigation. The timing of its publication could not be accidental, coming so soon after the lampooning of Jefferson for his own sexual adventures. Callender's incendiary *The Prospect Before Us*, published in 1800, harshly criticized the Washington and Adams administrations, which it characterized as aristocratic. The pamphlet ran to 187 pages. [43] Callender was indicted under the Sedition Act, but escaped to Ireland.

In response to Alien and Sedition Acts, Jefferson secretly authored, with James Madison, The Virginia and Kentucky Resolutions, which were read and accepted by the Virginia and Kentucky legislatures, respectively. The Resolutions called portions of the Acts unconstitutional, and restated the Jeffersonian principle of strict constructionism. However, the Resolutions went further, suggesting state nullification of unconstitutional federal laws, a position

Jefferson's adversaries certainly considered extreme, if not outright treasonous.

[I]t is true as a general principle, and is also expressly declared by one of the amendments to the Constitution that "the powers not delegated to the United States by the Constitution, nor prohibited by it to the states, are reserved to the states respectively or to the people;" and that no power over the freedom of religion, freedom of speech, or freedom of the press being delegated to the United States by the Constitution, nor prohibited by it to the states, all lawful powers respecting the same did of right remain, and were reserved to the states, or to the people: That thus was manifested their determination to retain to themselves the right of judging how far the licentiousness of speech and of the press may be abridged without lessening their useful freedom, and how far those abuses which cannot be separated from their use, should be tolerated rather than the use be destroyed; [44]

The lines were now firmly drawn. Vice President Jefferson, the Republican, was prepared to risk disunion rather than sacrifice the principles of liberty on which America had been founder. President Adams, the Federalist, was prepared to compromise principles in order to preserve the union. Jefferson's path was fraught with danger, calling for Americans to exercise their self-sufficiency as moral beings. Adams, on the other hand, offered security at a price very similar to that which the revolutionaries of his and Jefferson's generation had already decided was too high. Jefferson was proposing that good men could govern themselves, Adams that good men could govern other men. As the 18th Century drew to a close, Adams and Jefferson prepared to settle their dispute in a contentious election.

Leading up to this momentous event, a number of tragedies occurred in Jefferson's personal life. His sister Mary's marriage was on the rocks, victim of her husband's alcoholism. Sally Hemings had borne and lost two children:

Harriet Hemings, who lived two years, and an unnamed infant girl. Patsy wrote to her father of Harriet's death on January 22, 1798, blaming "the extreme dampness of the situation and an absolute want of offices of every kind to shelter the servants whilst in the performance of their duties" for an unprecedented outbreak of illness that claimed her baby sister. [45] If the loss inspired any special grief in Mr. Jefferson, it went unmentioned in his return letter. His silence should not be interpreted as callousness. He was not a callous man, but one accustomed to life's fragility.

The nation as a whole suffered a loss when George Washington died on December 14, 1799. No man had so perfectly embodied the American vision than the old General. Through his grim determination to cast off tyranny at any cost, Washington had inspired the American military force to stand together despite a critical lack of supplies, support, and that most important energy, hope. Not a brilliant strategist and far from the greatest orator of his age, the qualities that enabled him to lead were of a humbler sort. Steadfast under pressure, doggedly loyal, and courageous to a fault, he set an example that shamed less honest men.

To Jefferson, Washington had been both icon and adversary. More than any of the surviving Founding Fathers (Ben Franklin had died nine years earlier) Jefferson was in a position to look down on Washington as intellectually mundane. "His mind was great and powerful, without being of the very first order; ... no judgment was ever sounder," [46] Jefferson wrote years later. Washington's gift was not imagination, but conclusion. He was a man who sought counsel, and "selected what was best." Personally fearless, Jefferson selected prudence as "the strongest feature in his character". Never hasty, he refrained from acting, "until every circumstance, every consideration was maturely weighed." Washington pushed through "whatever obstacles opposed. His integrity was most pure, his justice the most inflexible I have ever known, no motives of interest or consanguinity, of friendship or hatred, being able to bias his decision. He was indeed, in every sense of the words, a wise, a good, & a great man."

This was no mere lip service. Having known George Washington for 30 years, Jefferson recognized in him a different sort of greatness than that which he strove after in his own life. Jefferson was a man of reason, Washington of action. Jefferson sought to bring conflicting impulses into harmony. Washington dispensed with contradiction as soon as he was able. In his will, Washington stipulated that all his slaves should be freed upon the death of his wife. This was a legally and financially difficult undertaking, unpopular with many of his relatives. Yet Washington followed through because he felt it was the right thing to do. Jefferson's blessing and curse was that he could not see the world in such simple terms: right and wrong, good and evil. His morality was complex. This complexity moved him to accept diverse opinions on governance, religion, and way of life as worthy of protection, informing his utopian vision of an actually and intellectually free society. At the same time, his constant rationalizing barred him from accepting the simple truth that he had once represented as his seminal conviction: that all men are created equal and entitled to their liberty.

The burning desire to obtain this liberty was brought home in dramatic fashion when a group of enslaved men including Gabriel Prosser, a blacksmith, conspired together to lead a violent uprising in early 1800. According to reports from fellow slaves who exposed the plot, the group intended to make a nighttime raid on nearby Richmond, Virginia. They planned to set fire to wooden buildings and use the distraction to cover their seizure of the city's armories, attacking white residents and any slaves who refused to join their side. Ultimately, they hoped to capture Governor James Madison, intending to hold him for ransom or perhaps execute him outright. Whatever the proposed fate of the Governor, the plan called for copious amounts of blood to be shed. Conspirator Jack Bowler, also a smith, confessed to forging fifty pikes, which would have been used alongside swords made from reshaped scythe blades. The plan also called for a large contingent of men. Sam Byrd Jr., generally considered the mastermind, claimed to have enlisted 500 volunteers. Other witnesses and confessors put the number much higher. [47]

The date was set for August 30. On that morning, a storm set in that captive James Callender described as, "the most terrible thunder Storm, accompanied with an enormous rain, that I have ever witnessed in this State." [48] Those conspirators near enough the appointed meeting place north of Richmond assembled, but the bulk of their force were stranded in the city by rain and floods. A young recruit named Pharoah, in service to the Sheppard household, observed the unraveling of the conspirators carefully laid plans. Perhaps fearing for his wife and son, Pharoah left the assembly and reported on the conspiracy to a fellow Sheppard slave named Tom. Tom reported immediately to his master, who passed on the information through a neighbor to the local captain of militia. In the raging storm, this man mounted an investigation, but was unable to discover any evidence of the raid moving forward. By this time, the conspirators had abandoned their original timeline. Thanks to the testimony of other slaves, the white men discovered that they planned now to attack on Sunday night. Governor James Monroe was informed, and the militia quickly brought in the principle conspirators.

After ten men had been convicted and hanged, Monroe sought the advice of Jefferson, his fellow Virginian, as to how long the executions should continue. Jefferson counseled mercy, if only for appearance's sake. "[T]he other states & the world at large will forever condemn us if we indulge a principle of revenge, or go one step beyond absolute necessity." [49] A further fifteen men, including Gabriel Prosser, went to the gallows. Pharoah and Tom were ultimately granted their freedom by acts of the state congress.

Chapter 13: Strange Bedfellows

The election of 1800 resulted in the most bizarre alliance of Jefferson's political life. Elections in New York State resulted in a Republican majority of electors, more-or-less cinching the presidential election in Jefferson's favor. The turnabout was largely due to the efforts of Aaron Burr. Burr had been a rival of Alexander Hamilton since 1791, when he was elected to the U. S. Senate by defeat of Hamilton's father-in-law Philip Schuyler. Though he lost the return contest six years later, Hamilton continued to watch Burr's accession through the Republican ranks with unease. After the New York election, Hamilton appealed to NY Governor John Jay to change the way the state chose its electors, but Jay refused to cater to party politics.

Burr's triumph put Hamilton in a particularly difficult political position. The course of the past four years had only served to deepen the divide between himself and the presidential incumbent.

One week before the opening of the electoral period on October 31st, he published his *Letter from Alexander Hamilton, Concerning the Public Conduct and Character of John Adams, Esq. President of the United States.* First affirming the "high veneration" he had once had for Adams, the document goes on to describe Hamilton's change in opinion, dating back all the way to his service under Washington in the Revolutionary War. Adams, says Hamilton, favored enlisting troops "annually, or for short periods, rather than for the term of the war" [50] and advocated replacing General Washington as Commander of the Army. Hamilton's attack was potent, given the messianic aura the late Washington had so recently attained. Pivoting from this, Hamilton went on to damn Adams by faint praise with regard to his involvement in negotiating aid from France and peace with Great Britain, giving the lion's share of credit for the latter to John Jay. He accused Adams of egotism and eccentricity, of conspiring against his friends and fellow Federalists. His thesis was that Adams was unworthy of the nation's highest office, and not to be trusted even by his own partisans.

As a remedy to being presented with candidates he could hardly stomach, Hamilton advocated splitting the Federalist vote between Adams and Charles Cotesworth Pinckney, brother to Thomas and a veteran of the XYZ Affair. He entertained some small hope that in the confusion, Pinckney might win the day. But it was not a hope he could cling to. In the end he decided it was better for the party to divorce themselves from the disastrous legacy of John Adams' presidency. "For my individual part my mind is made up," Hamilton wrote in a private letter in May of 1800, "I will never more be responsible for him by my direct support—even though the consequence should be the election of *Jefferson*. If we must have an *enemy* at the head of the Government, let it be one whom we can oppose & for whom we are not responsible, who will not involve our party in the disgrace of his foolish and bad measures. Under *Adams* as under *Jefferson* the government will sink. The party in the hands of whose chief it shall sink will sink with it and the advantage will all be on the side of his adversaries." [51] To save the ship of party, he was prepared to promote Jefferson to the captaincy of the nation.

By December of 1800, Jefferson was reasonably confident of Republican victory in the presidential contest. Electors had been popularly voted in from April to October, and it appeared clear what their ballots would say. The ballots themselves were opened for counting on February 11, 1801. As Vice President, Jefferson was empowered to read them out. A minor irregularity soon occurred. The ballots for Georgia were unsigned, rendering them technically invalid. Jefferson read out their content regardless, recording four votes for himself and four for Aaron Burr. [52] The final tally showed Jefferson and Burr tied at 73 ballots each, with 65 ballots for Adams, 64 for Pinckney, and 1 for John Jay. The Jay ballot had been a deliberate throwaway vote on the part of the Federalists, who hoped to give Adams the primacy. In contrast, the 73-73 tie forced the victorious Republicans to wait for the House of Representatives to decide which man, Jefferson or Burr, would become the third President of the United States of America.

We are accustomed to peaceful exchanges of power in our modern representative democracies. In 1801, the preponderance of historical evidence was in favor of violent dissolution. The succession of Oliver Cromwell's son Richard as Lord Protector had doomed the Commonwealth, and more recent examples in France were too terrible to contemplate. So it was to the Federalists' credit that they accepted the election's outcome with comparative grace. Still more surprising are the actions of Alexander Hamilton. Anticipating the impossible choice his colleagues would soon be facing, he encouraged Federalists members of the House to prepare to back Jefferson in the runoff. To the eventual defectors from the Federalist ranks he wrote, "To my mind a true estimate of Mr J.'s character warrants the expectation of a temporizing rather than a violent system. ... As to Burr these things are admitted and indeed cannot be denied, that he is a man of *extreme* & *irregular* ambition—that he is *selfish* to a degree which excludes all social affections & that he is decidedly *profligate*." [52] Once again, Hamilton revived his argument that backing the wrong man would do grave injury to the Federalist cause.

If the Antifœderalists who prevailed in the election are left to take their own man, they remain responsible, and the Fœderalists remain free united and without stain, in a situation to resist with effect pernicious measures. If the Fœderalists substitute Burr, they adopt him and become answerable for him. Whatever may be the theory of the case, abroad and at home (for so from the beginning will be taught) Mr Burr will become in fact the man of our party. And if he acts ill, we must share in the blame and disgrace. By adopting him we do all we can to reconcile the minds of the Fœderalists to him, and prepare them for the effectual operation of his arts. He will doubtless gain many of them, & the Fœderalists will become a disorganized and contemptible party.

James A. Bayard, recipient of this letter, switched his vote to Jefferson, deciding the election.

President Adams did not linger. His son Charles, a known drinker and reprobate, had died in the previous November. Adams was eager to take refuge from his troubles in the company of his family. He had, however, left his successor a dubious parting gift. The Judiciary Act of 1801 was meant to reduce the influence Republicans could hope to wield in the courts. It expanded the powers of the circuit courts and reduced the number of Supreme Court Justices by one.

Adams, the architect of checks and balances, hoped to prevent Republican domination of all three government branches. Twisting the knife, Adams nominated the staunchly Fedealist Secretary of State John Marshall for the position of Chief Justice. The appointment was swiftly ratified.

It was Marshall who presided at Jefferson's inauguration on Wednesday, March 4, 1801. The new president's address was designed to mend fences. Rumored to be an enemy of progress, he prefigured the concept of Manifest Destiny soon to take hold: "A rising nation, spread over a wide and fruitful land, traversing all the seas with the rich productions of their industry, engaged in commerce with nations who feel power and forget right, advancing rapidly to destinies beyond the reach of mortal eye; when I contemplate these transcendent objects, and see the honour, the happiness, and the hopes of this beloved country committed to the issue and the auspices of this day, I shrink from the contemplation & humble myself before the magnitude of the undertaking." [53] Speaking not of ethnic minorities, but of his own political foes, he continued,

All too will bear in mind this sacred principle, that though the will of the majority is in all cases to prevail, that will, to be rightful, must be reasonable; that the minority possess their equal rights, which equal laws must protect, and to violate would be oppression. ... [H]aving banished from our land that religious intolerance under which mankind so long bled and suffered, we have yet gained little if we countenance a political intolerance, as despotic, as wicked, and capable of as bitter and bloody persecutions.

"Every difference of opinion," asserted the champion of free speech, "is not a difference of principle." In waxing lyrical, he returned to his agrarian roots, but made a case for his vision with inclusive language.

[P]ossessing a chosen country, with room enough for our descendants to the thousandth and thousandth generation, entertaining a due sense of our equal right to the use of our own faculties, to the acquisitions of our own industry, to honor and confidence from our fellow citizens, resulting not from birth, but from our actions and their sense of them, enlightened by a benign religion, professed indeed and practised in various forms, yet all of them inculcating honesty, truth, temperance, gratitude and the love of man, acknowledging and adoring an overruling providence, which by all its dispensations proves that it delights in the happiness of man here, and his greater happiness hereafter; with all these blessings, what more is necessary to make us a happy and a prosperous people? Still one thing more, fellow citizens, a wise and frugal government, which shall restrain men from injuring one another, shall leave them otherwise free to regulate their own pursuits of industry and

improvement, and shall not take from the mouth of labor the bread it has earned. [54]

America would not be forever bounded by the Mississippi. In wresting from Great Britain a territory that had grown to more than four times the size of its parent country, the Americans had provided for the wealth and happiness of their posterity. What need had they of internal conflict, when they might rest peacefully from their long labor?

Chapter 14: Triumphs and Tribulations, Part One

President Jefferson began his term in office under the most desirable conditions imaginable. His party controlled the House and Senate. He had been voted in by a coalition of Southern and Northern states. The world was in an unusual period of peace, though those with an eye on Napoleon recognized this as the calm before the storm. Though the "Midnight Judges" appointed by the Judiciary Act were an annoyance, Jefferson quickly saw a way to lessen their impact. As Secretary of State, it had fallen to John Marshal to deliver the commissions of the 16 circuit judges and 42 justices of the peace appointed by the Act. This proved impossible in the time remaining to Marshal before his own transition into his role as Chief Justice. The commissions he left behind would have to be handed out by the incoming secretary.

Unlike Adams, who had carried over

Washington's cabinet into his administration, Jefferson decided to start with a clean slate. The ever loyal James Madison was to be Secretary of State, and Massachusetts representative Levi Lincoln the attorney general. While Madison made preparations, the president instructed Lincoln to refrain from distributing the remaining commissions. Madison continued this policy. Thus by simple laxity, the Federalist cause was held back until a more permanent solution could be found. In the meantime, Jefferson's new Secretary of the Treasury, Albert Gallatin, began a program to eliminate both the national debt and internal taxes. By Gallatin's estimation, the debt was approximately $83,000,000, being largely comprised of war debts to various creditors. Paying it down would require a sharp reduction in military spending, which had already begun during the last days of the Adams administration. Import tariffs were to furnish the federal government's income, while the states were expected to make ready their militias to defend against foreign attack.

Fears of a possible invasion became more pronounced in 1801, when rumor of a pending French acquisition of Western lands reached the president's ear. The United States' neighbor to the West had until this point in its history been Spain, specifically the Spanish Colony of Louisiana, which comprised a larger territory than that under U. S. control. The prospect of its transfer precipitated a crisis in U. S. foreign policy. Spain had been an idle neighbor, doing little to cultivate its interest in the West, and officially sanctioning U. S. use of the Mississippi River and the port of New Orleans. U. S. relations had only recently rebounded after the so-called Quasi-War due to the Adams administrations' mismanagement of foreign affairs. The Quasi-War had ended largely due to Napoleon's greater interest in European affairs. His move to secure the colony renewed fears of a powerful Old World empire exerting economic and territorial pressure.

A more pressing question of sovereign rights was opened when the pasha of Tripoli declared war on the United States on May 14, 1801. Pirates and slavers of the Barbary Coast had long preyed on the vessels of other nations who traded on the Mediterranean Sea, and coastal nations including Tripoli made regular demands for what amounted to protection money. Colonial vessels of the Americas had been under the protection of their respective nations, with France extending its protection to its allies during the Revolutionary War. But since 1785 U. S. ships had been viewed as an open target. Jefferson had already taken steps to end the threat posed by state-supported pirates by rallying the victim nations to form a naval coalition during his time as Minister to France. This effort had met with very limited success. In 1795, the U. S. agreed to pay tribute to Algiers, Tunis, and Tripoli in exchange for peace and the return of captured sailors. Pasha Yusuf Qaramanli complained of late payments and increased his demands. [55]

American was by no means a naval power. Before the declaration, Jefferson had dispatched three frigates and the schooner *Enterprise*, all under the command of Richard Dale with orders protect American shipping. [56] The effort was meant mainly to intimidate and inconvenience the pasha, rather than escalate the conflict. Commodore Dale even carried a letter promising further tribute if Qaramanli would conclude a peace. But upon arriving, Dale learned of the pasha's pronouncement and moved to blockade the enemy harbor, in line with his orders. On August 1, the *Enterprise* crippled the corsair *Tripolitan*. Its captain was "mounted on a Jack Ass (a saw horse) and paraded thro' the streets as an object of public scorn" and had the soles of his feet whipped by order of his chief. [57] It was the first major victory of a war that would last into Jefferson's second term, when Qaramanli agreed to return all American captives. The U. S. paid a ransom of $60,000 with the understanding that further tribute would not be owed.

As he waited on news from abroad, Jefferson continued to arrange his domestic affairs. He complained of being, "at a great loss, Mr. Madison not having been able to come on as yet, Mr. Gallatin not agreeing to join us till my return." [58] Jefferson got along with Gallatin, but more importantly, he got along with Gallatin's wife. Always fond of female company, he envisioned taking tea with Hannah Gallatin and Dolley Madison, as he had done with Abigail Adams, even while at odds with her husband. His most consistent pleasure was to be had in keeping his friends drawn close around him. A letter to daughter Polly reveals how far his thinking had changed from the days of his self-imposed hermitage from 1793-1797. He wrote, "I am convinced our own happiness requires that we should continue to mix with the world, & to keep pace with it as it goes; and that every person who retires from free communication with it is severely punished afterwards by the state of mind into which they get, and which can only be prevented by feeding our sociable principles." [59] Jefferson's only comfort in this time was sharing accomodations with his secretary Meriwether Lewis at the presidential mansion. Lewis's quarters occupied the East Room, as yet unfinished. Its walls were fashioned out of canvas.

In May of 1801 Jefferson heard that James Callender was in town. The imprisoned journalist had been promptly pardoned once Jefferson took office, but wished to have his $200 fine returned to him. Jefferson readily agreed, and sent word that he was pursuing the matter through official channels. This proved a source of difficulty, however, as Jefferson had already taken steps to remove the U. S. marshal who had collected Callender's fine, and who, in his view, was obligated to pay it back. The timing of the actions suggest no deliberate delay on Jefferson's part. He was responding to reports of jury packing (enlisting persons known to be biased for jury duty) in several jurisdictions, and only happened to scoop up the man in question. In yet another irony of his close knit community, the marshal was David Meade Randolph, brother-in-law to Jefferson's own son-in-law, Thomas Mann Randolph. In the same letter in which he complained of his isolation sans the company of Madison, Jefferson intimated to T. M. Randolph that the removal gave him "a great deal of pain". Callender's impatience would inspire an agony far greater.

But in 1801 and early 1802 there were still triumphs and joy in abundance. Two children were born to Jefferson's daughters in the fall. A convention was signed and ratified that officially put an end to the Quasi-War. Once again, the U. S. and France regarded each other as favored friends. The Judiciary Act of 1801 suffered repeal, further enraging Federalists. Congress approved Jefferson's plan for a U. S. Military Academy at West Point, NY. There was crisis as well, when Charles IV of Spain agreed to cede Louisiana to Napoleon, but with the restoration of normal diplomatic relations, Jefferson hoped for continued peace on the world stage. The greatest triumph of his presidency, and one of the greatest of his life, would follow from these proceedings.

Before that grand day came, however, he would be thrust once more into the fire of public scandal.

Chapter 15: The Case of Thomas Jefferson and Sally Hemings

Prior to 1998, a considerable amount of Jeffersonian scholarship was devoted to disproving the charges leveled against him by James Callender, as published in the *Richmond Recorder* of September 1, 1801 and thereafter. Even at the date of writing, the facts of the case are in dispute. Since the first rumblings of the scandal in 1796, through Callender's assertions and the later testimony of Madison Hemings, the story has served as a distraction both from the virtues and vices of Jefferson and his time. The moral lesson to be learned from its understanding exists in the circumstances surrounding the Sally Hemings tale more so than in its particulars. Still, it presents an opaque barrier beyond which those lessons can only dimly be perceived. It therefore behooves us to take a closer look at the evidence, both historical and scientific. Having come to consensus as to the probability or improbability of the affair, we will thereby be enabled to set its consideration aside, in favor of the larger issues of racism and its enmity towards freedom.

What were Callender's motivations in exposing (or concocting) the story? After he arrived in Washington in May 1801, the president dispatched Meriwether Lewis with an advance of $50 against the payment due him. But Callender's mind had already moved on. He demanded a political favor from Jefferson. The president was to use his influence to have Callender appointed postmaster of Richmond. In investigating the matter, James Madison reported to Governor Monroe that Callender "was under the tyranny of that of *love*", and that he hoped to secure his object thanks to the betterment his name would enjoy. [60] He pressed the matter, threatening to reveal Jefferson's support of his earlier attacks on the Federalists, Hamilton in particular. When Jefferson refused to be blackmailed, Callender followed through. Even after his fine was repaid, he continued to attack the president, his party, and his fellow newspapermen. He had fallen out with his former editor at the *Examiner*. He fell in with the editor of the *Recorder* in February 1802.

"The President, Again" was Callender's byline for his September 1st article. In it he repeated the basic charge published in the *Gazette of the United States* in 1796, enhanced with names and details. The most striking of these was that Jefferson's "concubine" had given him a son.

IT is well known that the man, whom it delighteth the people to honor, keeps, and for many years past has kept, as his concubine, one of his own slaves. Her name is SALLY. The name of her eldest son is TOM. His features are said to bear a striking although sable resemblance to those of the president himself. The boy is ten or twelve years of age. His mother went to France in the same vessel with Mr. Jefferson and his two daughters. The delicacy of this arrangement must strike every person of common sensibility. What a sublime pattern for an American ambassador to place before the eyes of two young ladies! [61]

One of Callender's facts was demonstrably wrong. Mary (Maria Jefferson, known as Polly) and Sally had not accompanied Jefferson to France but followed later. Another of his facts was proved wrong in 1998, as shortly to be discussed. Callender managed to correct his mistake about the timing of the girls' arrival before his death in 1803. But the basic accusation, that Jefferson had started a sexual relationship with Sally during his time in France, he let stand. "By this wench Sally, our president has had several children," Callender wrote. "There is not an individual in the neighbourhood of Charlottesville who does not believe the story; and not a few who know it." He mentions Jefferson's arguments that "belittle the African race", presumably a reference to *Notes on Virginia*, and concludes:

If the friends of Mr. Jefferson are convinced of his innocence, they will make an appeal of the same sort. If they rest in silence, or if they content themselves with resting upon a general denial, they cannot hope for credit. The allegation is of a nature too black to be suffered to remain in suspence. We should be glad to hear of its refutation. We give it to the world under the firmest belief that such a refutation never can be made. The African venus is said to officiate, as housekeeper at Monticello. When Mr. Jefferson has read this article, he will find leisure to estimate how much has been lost or gained by so many unprovoked attacks upon
J. T. CALLENDER

It's difficult to keep an open mind with Callender, as he struggles so hard to prejudice the reader against him. He was clearly an egotist of the first order. No passion for truth or justice spurred him on. He sought revenge for "unprovoked attacks". Callender's lack of credibility and his death the following year, which was ruled an accidental drowning, made it easy for Jefferson to ignore the accusations. His friends and supporters defended him, but he himself stayed silent. But was this a denial? The example of Alexander Hamilton had already proved to the public that where sex was concerned, libelous claims often had a germ of truth. Federalists continued to use the Sally scandal to attack Jefferson's character throughout his life, and his legacy after his death.

By 1873 Jefferson's Republican party had fractured and reformed. Now known as the Democratic Party, it opposed the party of Abraham Lincoln, which had taken on the Republican name. Thus, it was the *Pike County Republican* – a newspaper of the opposite party – that published Madison Hemings account of his mother and siblings in March of that year. In his account, Madison related the story of his mother accompanying Polly Jefferson to France.

According to his account, Sally Hemings knew her rights.

[Thomas Jefferson] desired to bring my mother back to Virginia with him but she demurred. She was just beginning to understand the French language well, and in France she was free, while if she returned to Virginia she would be re-enslaved. So she refused to return with him. To induce her to do so he promised her extraordinary privileges, and made a solemn pledge that her children should be freed at the age of twenty-one years. In consequence of his promise, on which she implicitly relied, she returned with him to Virginia. Soon after their arrival, she gave birth to a child, of whom Thomas Jefferson was the father. It lived but a short time. She gave birth to four others, and Jefferson was the father of all of them. Their names were Beverly, Harriet, Madison (myself), and Eston--three sons and one daughter. We all became free agreeably to the treaty entered into by our parents before we were born. [62]

Prior to the DNA evidence, the fact that Beverly, Harriet (the second girl of that name), Madison, and Eston Hemings were allowed to go free was the most credible argument for Jefferson's paternity. In total, Jefferson freed 10 of the 600 slaves he owned in his life. He gave manumission to two in his lifetime and five in his will. Three persons were allowed to run away without pursuit, an unusual practice for Jefferson, who caught and punished runaways, often selling repeat offenders. Of the ten total, five freed slaves were Sally's children. The rest were her brothers and nephews. The children ranged in age from 19-23 at the time of their gaining freedom. Beverly Hemings, at 23, ran away at the same time as his 21 year-old sister.

While this is certainly suggestive, it would be of little interest were it not for the Callender and Madison Hemings accusations. Historians might note it as a curiosity and wonder what special service these particular slaves had done to earn their freedom. One alternative was offered as an explanation of Madison and Eston's release, namely that they were to care for their uncle, John Hemings. John was a skilled woodworker who created many of the pieces at Monticello. His freedom was granted in the will, with a provision that he could remain at Monticello if he so chose, using the joinery and tools. He was also promised the help of assistants. Madison and Eston had been trained in cabinetry and other crafts by John, who continued to live and work at Monticello until the end of his life four years later.

An analysis of Jefferson's Farm Book, in which he recorded the day-to-day operations of Monticello, including his own visits, demonstrates that he was at home during every period when Sally Hemings became pregnant. This too is suggestive without being conclusive, as it is certainly possible that some other visitor, perhaps one who came on pretense of visiting Jefferson, was the father. Descendants of

Jefferson's acknowledged children implicated Peter and/or Samuel Carr, and elaborate confessions were published to this effect.

With so much contradictory leading, how are we to know whom to believe? James Callender certainly had another motive than truth-seeking when he published his dubious accounts. Madison Hemings did not, but the compiler of his recollections, Samuel F. Wetmore, may well have been swayed by partisanship, even at the remove of generations. So we must now ask, what did the DNA show?

The evidence depended on comparing the DNA of a known Jefferson descendant with someone definitely in the Hemings line. To this purpose, Dr. Eugene Foster compared the Y-chromosome of men from four family lines. The significant patriarchs of those lines were Field Jefferson, Eston Hemings, John Carr, and Thomas Woodson. Field Jefferson was Peter Jefferson's brother, therefore the paternal uncle of Thomas

Jefferson, who left no male heirs. John Carr was the grandfather of Peter and Samuel. Thomas Woodson was the supposed son of Jefferson and Hemings whom Madison claimed had died in infancy. Woodson family history asserted Callender's claim as to the identity of young Tom.

Had Field Jefferson's Y-chromosome had been shown to differ from that of Eston Hemings and Thomas Woodson, it would have conclusively proven that Thomas Jefferson (or his father, or his grandfather, or...) could not be the father of either man. Had John Carr's Y-chromosome been a match, it would have backed up the Jefferson family claim and supposed confessions. What Dr. Foster's study actually concluded was that Field Jefferson was of the same male genetic line as Eston Hemings, a line not shared by Carr or Woodson. The interpretation is that a Jefferson man almost definitely fathered Eston Hemings. Samuel or Peter Carr definitely did not. The parentage of

Thomas Woodson is a complete mystery, with father and mother both unknowns.

On the question of whether or not Thomas Jefferson, revolutionary and president, fathered one or all of his slave Sally Hemings' children, we cannot give a conclusive answer. Several Jefferson men have been suggested as alternative fathers. This is surely not a tactic Jefferson would have endorsed. Why should their names be sacrificed in defense of his own, by the mere conjecture? Thomas's younger brother Randolph Jefferson, accused of carrying on with Sally, had his own slaves. Why should he not have confided his infidelity to his own house? Certainly it was more convenient to Jefferson's visitors to find concubines from among women who were considered their own property. In the winking planter culture, where a man was entitled to make whatever use he pleased of his human chattel, would it not have been the height of indecency to make such use of the chattel of another man without his consent?

It is supposed by his defenders that Thomas Jefferson was not a man like other men. That he stood apart from his contemporaries, and indeed, from man of any time. Certainly he must have been a saint to honor the wish of his deceased wife that he should not remarry, even after his daughters had grown and taken husbands of their own. It seems hard to credit that Martha Wayles Skelton Randolph, who herself had two husbands, expected the man who outlived her to remain celibate for the 44 years following her death. Surely Thomas Jefferson, man of reason, would not have interpreted her stricture as binding once the cause for said stricture – Martha's own experiences as a step-daughter – no longer had relevance. That he did not marry was a choice. That he had the normal urges of a healthy man he demonstrated by Martha's frequent pregnancies. How then did he channel those urges?

Those who elevate Thomas Jefferson above the

stature of common men do so without his consent. He held sacred and undeniable that all men are equal. His life demonstrates that his actual belief was that men born free are equal, while persons born in slavery were destined to be dominated. None could ever prove to him that the African-Americans then comprising the slave class were an exception to this flawed premise. Not Benjamin Banneker, nor Sally, nor the children they had together. To have changed his belief would have obligated to take up the abolitionist cause. He was sure the union could not survive the struggle abolition required. And so his silence must be seen for what it was, the decision to favor the nation he had brought forth over his natural offspring.

Chapter 16: Trials and Tribulations, Part Two

If Callender's accusations stung, Jefferson rebounded from them quickly. Christmas 1802 was an especially festive time, with both Jefferson daughters paying visits. Early in 1803 he turned his mind to serious matters, appointing James Monroe as special envoy to France. Reports from the minister abroad had confirmed the urgency of the times. That Napoleon was preparing for war in Europe was not news, but he appeared to be accelerating his timetable. The Emperor himself hinted as much to the British envoy, in the hearing of witnesses. This prospect presented Jefferson with an opportunity.

France already had mixed feelings about its colonial possessions. Since 1791 its interest in the New World had been tainted by the slave rebellion on St. Domingue. So terrible were the conditions in the French sugar plantations that slave workers were unable to reproduce in significant numbers. By 1789, an annual supply of 30,000 replacement slaves were being shipped in. The Haitian Revolution, as it came to be called, happened in stages. After overthrowing the colonial government and announcing the abolishment of slavery, self-declared Governor-General Toussaint L'Ouverture initially offered his allegiance to France, with the understanding that he would rule the island essentially as an independent state. Napoleon responded by sending an expeditionary force that captured L'Ouverture but were subsequently devastated by an outbreak of yellow fever. A renewed rebellion, spurred by the revelation that the French intended to re-institute slavery, threw off the French yoke once and for all. The cost in men and gold convinced Napoleon to renounce Louisiana.

Foreign Minister Talleyrand negotiated with James Monroe and Robert Livingston for the sale of the entire territory, which Jefferson underestimated at 500 million acres. The U. S. at that time comprised 434 million acres. France's price was a mere $15 million, only a third more than the U. S. had been prepared to offer for New Orleans alone. The deal was better than Jefferson had hoped to dream. To even contemplate refusal was unthinkable.

Jefferson considered asking Congress for a Constitutional amendment granting themselves the power to purchase land from foreign nations. Speed, however, was of the essence. Monroe and Livingston warned that Napoleon might rescind the offer. There was also danger that the Northern States would object to the diffusion of their power. Setting aside his strict constructionist scruples, Jefferson pushed for speedy acceptance. The Louisiana Purchase Treaty was ratified on October 20, 1803. One of the first correspondents Jefferson informed was Meriwether Lewis, whom he had commissioned earlier in the year to make a journey of exploration into the West. Lewis and his companions in the Corps of Discovery had just met with William Clark's group at the Falls of Ohio. With Louisiana in American hands and the expedition underway, the Western march of U. S. expansion, along with the consequent suppression of Native American tribes, was practically a *fait accompli*.

Entering his third year as president, Jefferson's popularity among the masses was unassailable. His Federalist enemies ground their teeth. In one of the astounding reversals of which political history is fond, they had reason to fear a Jeffersonian dynasty, the permanent investment of authority in the hands of their enemy and his political sons. The first fence post that would defend against this phantasmagorical tyranny had already been installed, however. In February of 1803, the Supreme Court under Chief Justice Marshall had heard the case of Marbury vs. Madison. William Marbury had been appointed by the Adams administration as Justice of the Peace for the District of Columbia, but in keeping with Jefferson's policy, Madison had withheld his commission. Marbury's suit tested the power of the Executive to refuse to enforce legislative decrees and of the Judiciary to dictate to the Executive. The opinion handed down by Marshall was ingenious. Marbury's request for a writ of mandamus commanding the Secretary of State to deliver his commission was denied, on the basis that the original Judiciary Act of 1789 (which the 1801 Act modified) was unconstitutional. It assigned power to issue writs to the Supreme Court, a power not found in the founding text.

This reversal of Federalist and Republican roles, with Federalist Marshall arguing for a strict interpretation of the Constitution's mandate to the courts, established the concept of judicial review. The Judicial branch would be the arbiter of Constitutional authority by appeal to that authority. Rather than the other two branches being free to interpret the Constitution for themselves, the courts would provide redress whenever boundaries were tested. Jefferson objected, suggesting that the judges of the courts would inevitably use this new authority to impose oligarchical rule. In this way he returned the debate to its partisan framing, with Republicans as the defenders against Federalist despotism. But in this criticism he missed the point. Marshall was only at a slight remove from John Adams as an engineer of checks and balances. By asserting the Judiciary's right to review, he did much to ensure that rule by the populous would not be absolute. An anti-democratic sentiment, perhaps, but one that strengthened the republic.

That strength was tested in 1804 by the self-serving actions of Vice President Burr and the fractious talk of Jefferson's Federalist opposition. In January, Burr visited the president, whom he had scarcely seen since the election. His silence during the run off balloting had been interpreted by Jefferson as a power grab. That it failed did nothing to endear Burr to the president, who informed Burr that he would not ask the party to pair them as running mates in the next election. This refusal was still more infuriating because the 12th Amendment to the Constitution eliminated the practice of awarding the vice presidency to the second-place holder. Without Jefferson's blessing, Burr would be shut out.

In February, Senator Timothy Pickering of Massachusetts began to agitate for the Northern States to secede from the Union. This precipitated a split in the Federalists. Pickering's faction, known as Essex Junto, backed Aaron Burr in the 1804 New York gubernatorial election, despite Burr's nominal Republicanism. Opposed to Northern secession, Jefferson's old nemesis Alexander Hamilton threw his support behind Morgan Lewis, the orthodox Republican candidate. Burr blamed Hamilton for his subsequent loss. After Hamilton made a scathing denouncement of the failed candidate at a dinner party, Burr challenged him to a duel.

Then a fading practice among the gentry, duels of this sort were meant to defend honor, not result in death, and both combatants had participated in them before. In a letter written the night before the duel, Hamilton took an oath not to fire at his opponent. Though Burr took no such oath, he may well have intended to fire into the ground, and been startled when Hamilton discharged his own pistol into the trees. Whatever the case, Burr did shoot, and his musket ball did mortal damage to Hamilton's viscera. The great foe and occasional ally of the President lingered on until the next day, then died at the age of 49.

Jefferson said nothing about his rival's death. He may have felt it prudent to keep his peace; he may also still have been mourning a personal loss. Five years earlier, the death of Jefferson's unacknowledged daughter, Harriet, had preceded the nation loss of George Washington. In April of 1804, Maria Jefferson Eppes, his darling Polly, had died. Typically, he kept his deep feelings out of his correspondence, but friends and family noted it and wrote it down. The bitterness of the loss even inspired Abigail Adams to take up writing to Jefferson again, setting aside feelings of resentment about the rift between Jefferson and her husband. When their conversation returned to partisan topics some months later, she broke off the communication yet again. The two most famous Founding Fathers left alive had been driven so far apart that even commiseration had to make way for politics.

Chapter 17: A Failure of Ideals

The Federalists ran Charles Cotesworth Pinckney as their candidate for president in 1804. He carried 14 electoral votes to Jefferson's 162. No one thought Pinckney a threat to the president. This was through no fault of his own. With the country safe and prosperous and twice the size it had been before his administration, Jefferson governed modestly, with the full swell of public mandate at his back. In his second inaugural address, he expressed his hopes for a continued, prosperous peace.

Contemplating the union of sentiment now manifested so generally, as auguring harmony and happiness to our future course, I offer to our country sincere congratulations. With those, too, not yet rallied to the same point, the disposition to do so is gaining strength; facts are piercing through the veil drawn over them; and our doubting brethren will at length see, that the mass of their fellow citizens, with whom they cannot yet resolve to act, as to principles and measures, think as they think, and desire what they desire; that our wish, as well as theirs, is, that the public efforts may be directed honestly to the public good, that peace be cultivated, civil and religious liberty unassailed, law and order preserved; equality of rights maintained, and that state of property, equal or unequal, which results to every man from his own industry, or that of his fathers. When satisfied of these views, it is not in human nature that they should not approve and support them; in the meantime, let us cherish them with patient affection; let us do them justice, and more than justice, in all competitions of interest; and we need not doubt that truth, reason, and their own interests, will at length prevail, will gather them into the fold of their country, and will complete their entire union of opinion, which gives to a nation the blessing of harmony, and the benefit of all its strength. [63]

The invitation for those who had "not yet rallied to the same point" of political unity to do so was a departure from his first message, in which he decried the need for labels and parties when all were Americans were simultaneously federalists and republicans in their common interests. There was no need to wash away the political distinctions of friend and foe. The people themselves had washed them away. Jefferson had won the war and extended the olive branch to his foes.

The war in Tripoli was satisfactorily concluded in September 1805, though Congress did not ratify its treaty until the next year. In November the Corp of Discovery reached the Pacific Ocean. Though they had not found a water route across the North American continent, the Lewis and Clark expedition had achieved Jefferson's prescient ambition. Their adventure would inspire the Westward expansion which he foresaw as defining the next great era of the American experiment. Long before the joyous news of the achievement reached the nation, however, Jefferson's Republican party followed the example of their Federalist foes in generating splinter groups. The criticism of John Randolph of Roanoke, Representative from Virginia, sparked a movement towards an extreme affirmation of State's rights within a group that came to be called the Old Republicans, or Quids. Randolph charged that Jefferson had betrayed the party by expanding the powers of the central government. This was something he certainly had done in the case of the Louisiana Purchase. Randolph discounted the pragmatism of Jefferson's policies, faulting him for compromising Republican ideals.

One of Jefferson's fondest associations came to an abrupt end in 1806. George Wythe, his old teacher of law, died suddenly and under suspicious circumstances. Hit autopsy concluded that the 79 or 80 year-old Wythe had been poisoned. Nineteen years previous, Wythe had become a widower, and promptly freed a number of his slaves. Some of the free blacks chose to remain in his service, among them a woman named Lydia Broadnax. Wythe, Broadnax, and Broadnax's son Michael Brown all became ill at one time, and Wythe and Brown both died within days. The poisoner was found to be Wythe's own grand-nephew, George Sweeney. Sweeney was in line to inherit some of Wythe's estate, as were Broadnax and Brown. When the case was brought to trial, Broadnax and other black servants testified to seeing Sweeney lurking around the coffee pot from which the victims all drank. Since Virginia law did not permit a black person to testify against whites, their testimony was disallowed, and Sweeney acquitted. In his will, George Wythe requested his famous student, Thomas Jefferson, to personally attend to the 16 year-old Michael Brown's education. Informed of these proceedings, Jefferson commented, "I sincerely regret the loss of the [Michael Brown] not only for the affliction it must have cost Mr. Wythe in his last moments, but also as it has deprived me of an object for attentions which would have gratified me unceasingly with the constant recollection and execution of the wishes of my friend." [64]

While Jefferson was mourning his friend, American fears of a renewed conflict with Britain were moving closer to realization. Britain was ramping up for war against Napoleon, and during an eager search for deserters, the captain of HMS *Leander* fired a warning shot in New York harbor that decapitated sailor John Pierce. The incident resulted in a public outcry for the captain to be brought to justice. President Jefferson commanded that *Leander* and her sister ships leave U. S. waters. Back in England, Captain Henry Whitby was acquitted on a charge of murder. Tensions between the two countries reached a fever pitch in June of 1807 when the HMS *Leopard* opened fire on the U. S. frigate *Chesapeake* after the latter refused to be boarded. Three men were killed and several wounded. *Leopard* had been hunting for three sailors, who although citizens of the U. S., had enlisted in and then fled from the British Royal Navy. The request to have the men handed over had already been refused by Secretary of State Madison on the grounds that Britain was at war with France, with the U. S. a declared neutral party. Now *Leopard* had committed an act of war that threatened to draw them in on the French side.

How would Jefferson react? The country was certainly not a match for British military might, but Napoleon was quite a distraction. A show of American resolve might persuade the revolutionary foe that their interests were best served by staying close to home. An invasion of British-held Canada was suggested. Jefferson issued a decree banning all British vessels from American waters, save for those involved in official business, and wrote letters to the governors to furnish a militia of 100,000 men. Though he had acted peremptorily, Congress approved the measure. In a bold stroke of political theater, Jefferson sent the USS *Revenge* to London with diplomatic orders for James Monroe. The orders demanded that Britain leave off the impressing of American sailors. They also called for the return of the sailors seized by the *Leopard*. Four men had been taken off the Chesapeake, including the three Americans and one man known to be a British subject. Negotiations continued until 1811, when the two surviving Americans were freed.

While the Chesapeake-Leopard Affair was playing out on the high seas, ex-Vice President Aaron Burr was facing trial on charges of treason. Wanted for murder in New York, Burr had spent the spring and summer of 1805 traveling in the South and West of the country. Rumors abounded that he intended to make an alliance with Mexican separatists and help liberate the Spanish colony. Whether he meant to set himself up as a dictator or hand the territory over to the federal government to cash in its political capital is still a matter of debate among scholars, but whatever his plan, by November of the next year, Burr had been positively identified as the leader of a conspiracy. Through various agents, he had been recruiting a private military force. He had also attempted to persuade General James Wilkinson, Governor of the Louisiana Territory, to join his cause. New Orleans and Louisiana would fall to Burr and Wilkinson, then they would press on into Mexico, Burr promised. After some deliberation, Wilkinson revealed the plot, and the president sent letters to the governors to watch for and apprehend Burr.

Jefferson himself undertook to explain the plot to Congress. He found it difficult, so fraught with intrigue had been of Burr's machinations. He wrote that Burr "contemplated two distinct objects, which might be carried on either jointly or separately, and either the one, or the other first as circumstances should direct. One of these was the severance of the union of these states by the Alleganey mountains; the other an attack on

Mexico." [65] Finding that the secession of the Western states "could not be effected with the consent of its inhabitants, & that his resources were inadequate, as yet, to effect it by force he took his course then at once, determined to seize on N. Orleans, plunder the bank there, possess himself of the Military & Naval stores, and proceed on his expedition to Mexico." The plan did not coalesce. Alarmed by Jefferson's call for his apprehension, Burr cut his losses, surrendering to authorities in Mississippi. He later escaped custody, but was taken again in Alabama.

Had his trial been televised, it would have rivaled any modern media circus. The case against Aaron Burr seemed damning to the president, but it depended on conjecture and hearsay. Chief Justice Marshal presided. The venue was the Fifth Circuit Court in Richmond, Virginia. Defendant Burr requested that President Jefferson be issued a subpeona *duces tecum*, bringing along with him the letter from

Wilkinson that exposed the plot. The president, however, was unable to find the letter, and explained that he could not come himself to Richmond due to the demands of the presidential office. Within a week the Chesapeake was fired upon, justifying his refusal. When Wilkinson himself could not locate the original letter from which the president's copy had been made, he attempted to submit yet another copy in its place. Burr's legal team refused to accept this substitution. The coded letter Burr had used to solicit Wilkinson was admitted as evidence. Even this was not enough to convince the jury that Burr was guilty of treason. The complex ephemeral nature of the conspiracy, which no witness could explain in its entirety, helped Burr's case. He had not factually invaded New Orleans or anywhere else, and the Constitution defined treason against the United States as "levying war against them, or in adhering to their enemies, giving them aid and comfort." Rumors of Burrs involvement with Spanish revolutionaries and his own (evidently dishonest) assertions that Great Britain was prepared to send ships to his aid was not enough. "No person shall be convicted of treason unless on the testimony of two witnesses to the same overt act, or on confession in open court" asserted the nation's defining text. On September 1, 1807 Burr was pronounced not guilty.

Jefferson felt that Justice Marshall had mismanaged the trial. "[W]e had supposed we possessed fixed laws to guard us equally against treason & oppression. But it now appears we have no law but the will of the judge. Never will chicanery have a more difficult task than has been now accomplished to warp the text of the law to the will of him who is to construe it." [66] There was no solution to the quandary, as any attempt to amend the Constitution would be equally open to scrutiny by the courts. Once again Jefferson feared that tyranny would overcome the precepts of freedom he cherished. But his perception was hardly without bias. His own authority had been challenged, and he found himself in the unenviable position of being reckoned the equal of every man under law.

Turning back to the larger question of the day, Jefferson consulted with Albert Gallatin about how America should take its stand against Great Britain. Following along from the *Chesapeake-Leopard Affair*, the Privy Council of the United Kingdom had issued Orders in Council that forbade neutral powers from trading with France, and instituted a blockade. Jefferson's wished to respond in kind, issuing an embargo against the buying and selling of British goods. Any alternative, he feared, would require the United States to take sides in the European war. Gallatin saw the argument, but was concerned about the effects of a lengthy embargo.

[A]n embargo, for a limited time will at this moment be preferable in itself & less objectionable in Congress. In every point of view, privations, sufferings, revenue, effect on

the enemy, politics at home &c., I prefer war to a permanent embargo. Governmental prohibitions do always more mischief than had been calculated; and it is not without much hesitation that a statesman should hazard to regulate the concerns of individuals as if he could do it better than themselves. [67]

Even granted the high cost of a military confrontation, Gallatin feared that an embargo would be more costly still. He may have wondered if Jefferson would be attracted to the idea for reasons of nostalgia. It had been the Virginia Burgesses' decision to accept no goods from the mother country that had launched Jefferson into the revolutionary sphere. His agrarian sympathies, the store he put by self-sufficiency, and his national pride might skew the president's assessment of the balance scales. While America represented a significant market for British finished goods manufacturers, the UK was not so dependent on American products that their restriction would create panic in the

Houses of Parliament.

The Embargo Act was passed in December 1807. It forbade American vessels from entering foreign ports and foreign vessels from leaving port while loaded with American goods. By restricting all foreign trade, America was in effect honoring the UK Orders in Council and Napoleon's decrees forbidding trade with Great Britain (those these applied only in Europe), further emphasizing the States' neutrality. Two further Acts restricted river, coastal and overland trade, closing loopholes that traders had been exploiting by carrying goods to and from British Canada and Spanish Florida.

The response to these restrictions was an outbreak of lawlessness. The scope of this rebellion was so wide that Jefferson issued a proclamation on April 19, 1808, which said in part,

I do hereby further require and command all

officers having authority civil or military, and all other persons civil or military who shall be found within the vicinage of such insurrections or combinations, to be aiding and assisting by all the means in their power by force of arms or otherwise to quell and subdue such insurrections or combinations, to seize upon all those therein concerned who shall not instantly and without delay disperse and retire to their respective abodes, and to deliver them over to the civil authority of the place to be proceeded against according to law. [68]

Northern traders were openly flouting the Acts provisions, and Jefferson felt it necessary to remind local officials of their responsibility to enforce the law. Many in his own party opposed him, with Republicans arguing for nullification at the state level. In contrast, John Quincy Adams, son of Jefferson's estranged friend, was ostracized by the Federalists for support of the embargo. The Senator from Massachusetts resigned his seat and switched parties. Jefferson was ridiculed in poetry and prose. A popular song of the time, written by a thirteen year-old Federalist, likened the embargo to a turtle shell in which the president and his political allies hid themselves. To men who made their living on the sea, Jefferson seemed to have chosen war with them over war with a foreign power. During the annual presidential retreat of 1808, a letter writing campaign centered in Massachusetts and attributed to Essex Junto deluged Monticello with up to 50 protests a day.

Was the embargo a uniquely inelegant political failure on the part of Jefferson? In assessing its worth, we must attempt to see it from Jefferson's perspective. For him its estimation was always that of a necessary preventative against an unwinnable war.

The embargo keeping at home our vessels, cargoes & seamen, saves us the necessity of making their capture the cause of immediate war: for if going to England, France had determined to take them, if to any other place, England was to take them. Till they return to some sense of moral duty therefore, we keep within ourselves. This gives time. Time may produce peace in Europe. Peace in Europe removes all causes of differences till another European war, & by that time our debt may be paid, our revenues clear, & our strength increased. [69]

His own assessment of the economic bounties to come was overly optimistic, but he believed wholeheartedly that "moral duty" would eventually compel the European nations to involve themselves once more in peaceful commerce. It seems an odd supposition from a man who had rebelled against the immoral tyranny of imperial powers, but he was, as has been stated, an idealist.

Though Jefferson's popularity had plummeted in the North, partisan loyalty and the more agrarian nature of the Southern economy sustained his successor through the election of 1808. James Madison took 122 electoral votes, to the recurrent C. C. Pinckney's 49. News from abroad was less cheering. Britain and France responded hardly at all to the American insistence on neutrality and the cessation of trade. Resistance to the embargo, the nature of the markets, and the timing of transatlantic travel meant that this was not accurately assessed until after the election. Confronting the economic reality, but still apprehensive about losing neutral status, Congress passed the Non-Intercourse Act, permitting trade with all countries except Britain and France, whose ships it barred from U. S. waters. Jefferson signed the Act on March 1, 1809, one of his last acts in office. He attended the first inaugural ball, in honor of President Madison, and lingered at the presidential mansion for a few days before departing for Monticello.

Chapter 18: The Finished Legacy

Monticello was a paradise for Jefferson, the home he had always longed for, where he could gather his family for books, take walks with the children, and preside over farm and household matters. He took daily rides of several hours on horseback, indulged in his books, and tinkered endlessly with various inventions. One of these was a rotating conveyance for his shirts that resided in his wardrobe. In Monticello he had peace and prosperity, the rewards of a life lived in public service.

And always, there were his slaves. Unsympathetic visitors remarked on the obvious similarity between his own features and those of several children of the house, reviving the 1802 story of "Black Sal". Years later, the oldest Jefferson grandson, Thomas Randolph Jefferson, admitted the resemblance to the patriarch's biographers, relating an anecdote in which "a gentleman dining with Mr. Jefferson, looked so startled as he raised his eyes from the latter to the servant behind him, that his discovery of the resemblance was perfectly obvious to all." [70] T. R. Jefferson claimed that his uncle, Peter Carr, was the father of Sally Heming's children, which as has been discussed, was disproved in 1998. The fact that he gave his testimony in defense of his grandfather's reputation makes it all the more credible. Even at so far a remove as 1868, and with his half-brother Madison's account yet to be added to the historical debate, grandson Thomas evidently believed that the biographers would find too strong a tradition of a family resemblance to easily dismiss. So he repeated the family lie, a lie he may well have believed.

Starting in 1811, the two ex-presidents whose friendship had been sacrificed to partisan struggles, Jefferson and Adams, carried on a renewed correspondence. Friends had conveyed complimentary remarks by Jefferson to Adams. Recounting Adams' response, Jefferson wrote, "'I always loved Jefferson, and still love him'—this is enough for me. I only needed this knowledge to revive towards him all the affections of the most cordial moments of our lives." [71] He despised the divisive effects of partisanship. In making peace with Adams he defied its power, proving that he was motivated by higher ideals.

All was not horseback rides and dinner parties, though these consumed large portions of his days. The outbreak of war in 1812 brought back his worst fears. Would the American experiment end in re-conquest and the ultimate triumph of monarchy? Despite the military failures of the war, its conclusion in 1815 signaled to Jefferson and the world that the United States could defend its interests, and did much to ensure its continued independence. The war's aftermath also signaled the end of the Federalist party, which had argued for the breaking of the Union. Secure in hopes for a prosperous future, American voters showed their confidence in Republicanism by electing James Monroe as fifth president in an 1816 landslide.

Closer to home, Jefferson's happiness was interrupted by the disgraceful drunkenness of his grandson-in-law. Ann Cary Randolph had married Charles Bankhead in 1791. The couple moved next door to Monticello in 1811, but Bankhead soon proved incompetent with the family finances, and their home plantation of Carlton was handed over to trustees. When in drink, Bankhead was belligerent and dangerous. Ann spent much of her married life fleeing from his rages. His violence extended to attempted murder. In 1819 he assaulted T. J. Randolph, stabbing his nephew twice. The 76 year-old Jefferson galloped four miles from Monticello to knell beside his grandson, weeping. Is it any wonder that Randolph, upon surviving, went on to defend his grandfather's name?

At the same time he was fighting to resolve his family troubles, Jefferson worked towards securing the last great piece of his legacy. For the better part of forty years he had hoped to found a University. In 1816, Jefferson's plan for a Central College was approved by the Virginia Assembly, and in 1817 the first meeting of the Board of Visitors was held. Jefferson himself took the minutes, with Presidents Madison and Monroe both present. A location for the College was chosen. In 1819, the renamed University of Virginia received its charter. As first rector, Jefferson oversaw construction, following his own architectural designs. In 1825 Jefferson began hosting Sunday dinners at Monticello for the first student class.

Age had taken its toll. His tall frame had begun to stoop. He complained of being able to read only one newspaper and day, and forgetting the contents soon after. Mounting a horse involved standing on a platform or terrace above the animal and settling himself down onto its back. An intestinal complaint that he had first reported to his doctor in 1801 slowly drained him of vitality. On June 24, 1826 he summoned Dr.

Robley Dunglison, UVA professor of anatomy and medicine, from Charlottesville. Jefferson met his guest in the parlor, and was then confined to his bed. Under the care of the good doctor, he was determined to survive ten days more, to die on the 4th of July. The struggle was long and bitter. Dunglinson administered laudanum in a dose that had proved effective against earlier attacks, but it was soon clear that there would be no last-second recovery. At nine p.m. on the 3rd, he refused a proffered dose. Dreams of flight and fear assailed him, and he was heard to say, "Warn the Committee to be on the alert," according to his grandson. This would have been the Virginia Committee of Correspondence, proposed by his late friend Dabney Carr and co-founded by Jefferson in 1773 to sow the seeds of revolution.

On July 4th, 1826 at 12:50 in the afternoon, Thomas Jefferson died. In accord with his Enlightenment beliefs, he had long refused to classify himself as a member of any orthodox

Christian sect. Of the Trinity teaching he wrote, "it is too late in the day for men of sincerity to pretend they believe in the Platonic mysticisms that three are one, & one is three; & yet the one is not three, and the three are not one". [72] Yet he was no atheist, and on his deathbed he proclaimed his hope of an afterlife. In a chest that he had instructed her not to open until after his death, he had left his last surviving daughter, Patsy, a short poem.

Life's visions are vanished, its dreams are no more.
Dear friends of my bosom, why bathed in tears?
I go to my fathers; I welcome the shore,
which crowns all my hopes, or which buries my cares.
Then farewell my dear, my lov'd daughter, Adieu!
The last pang of life is in parting from you!
Two Seraphs await me, long shrouded in death:
I will bear them your love on my last parting breath. [73]

And so came to an end one of the most storied lives in American history, fifty years after his great document had been signed and the experiment in liberty had begun in earnest. Five hours later and 550 miles away, John Adams died. His last words were, "Thomas Jefferson survives."

Chapter 19: A Great Man

And so we come once again to the question of Thomas Jefferson's greatness. More than any of the Founding Fathers, he dreamt of a better tomorrow, envisioned a freer, happier society and worked whole-souled to see that dream realized. As a contributor to modern political thought, he is without peer. Yet Jefferson had a weakness, in that his racial attitudes blinded him to the need to use his considerable political talent to work to eliminate the blight of slavery. When it came to his personal affairs he was an ordinary man – painfully ordinary, from the perspective of his defenders. His moral compass inclined to the same pole as that of the mass of his contemporaries. He believed in a natural hierarchy, an unequal birth, the destiny of some people to be dominated by others, and he indulged his own instinct to dominate.

One of Jefferson's last major political statements was on the subject of slave states vs. free states.

The 1819 Missouri Compromise troubled him greatly. Proposed by Senator Henry Clay, the plan admitted Missouri as a slave state while creating Maine as a free state by a division of Massachusetts, and prohibited slavery in new states geographically positioned above 36°30' latitude. The imposition of a boundary line was a potentially fatal mistake according to Jefferson. He wrote to Maine Senator John Holmes in response to Holmes' pamphlet lauding the compromise:

I had for a long time ceased to read newspapers or pay any attention to public affairs, confident they were in good hands, and content to be a passenger in our bark to the shore from which I am not distant. But this mementous question, like a fire bell in the night, awakened and filled me with terror. I considered it at once as the knell of the Union. ... a geographical line, coinciding with a marked principle, moral and political, once concieved and held up to the angry passions of men, will never be *obliterated; and every new irritation will mark it deeper and deeper. I can say with conscious truth that there is not a man on earth who would sacrifice more than I would, to relieve us from this heavy reproach, in any <u>practicable</u> way. the cession of that kind of property, for it is so misnamed, is a bagatelle which would not cost me a second thought, if, in that way, a general emancipation and <u>expatriation</u> could be effected: and, gradually, and with due sacrifices, I think it might be. but, as it is, we have the wolf by the ear, and we can neither hold him, nor safely let him go. justice is in one scale, and self-preservation in the other. ... I regret that I am now to die in the belief that the useless sacrifice of themselves, by the generation of '76. to acquire self government and happiness to their country, is to be thrown away by the unwise and unworthy passions of their sons, and that my only consolation is to be that I live not to weep over it. if they would but dispassionately weigh the blessings they would throw away against an abstract principle more* *likely to be effected by union than by scission, they would pause before they would perpetrate this act of suicide on themselves and of treason against the hopes of the world.* [74]

A death knell in the night, a quote from Suetonius, and a Founder's regret for the unworthiness of a new generation. With such poetry does Jefferson confront the problem that we are inclined to credit his argument, even as we are aware of his vested interest. The slaves of Monticello fed him, clothed him, and provided every comfort he delighted in extending to family and friends. He could not credit that once emancipated, as he imagined their children or grandchildren would be, that former slaves could live as free Americans. He did not ask how they wished to live, or where, or what was owed them. As he wished to do with his considerable debt, he wanted the debt of white Americans wiped away, the slate cleaned. Freedom would start with exile and abandonment. Any other path would end in national suicide.

He loved America. Threatening its union was "treason against the hopes of the world." That world was comprised of persons who had been born to freedom but made subject to tyranny by priests and kings. The Enlightenment had shown the oppressed a dream of liberty, and the United States was the realization of that dream. But he did not believe the immortal words, "all men are created equal". Some men were born subservient. This was a fact of nature, Jefferson had argued in *Notes on the State of Virginia*, easily discernible by the deficiencies in black souls. He clung to this pronouncement despite a lifetime of intimate connections with the Hemings family. James Hemings had brought French cooking to America. Sally Hemings had satisfied his most personal and private need. The children of their union were house slaves or assistants to their uncle John, whose beautifully crafted furniture is still on display at Monticello.

It was John Hemings who fashioned the coffin

that Wormley Hughes, slave gardener and hostler and a nephew of Sally Hemings, lowered into the ground. Sally herself was not freed by Jefferson's will but released by Patsy into the care of her sons. Eight years later she was "given her time". Virginia law required freed slaves to quit the state within one year, so this informal release permitted her to remain. According to her son Madison, Sally Hemings lived with him and his brother Eston until her death in 1835. Eston moved to Ohio where he became a celebrated musician, well-known for his skill with the violin. His son enlisted in the Union army, serving as a Colonel in the Civil War. Madison and his family joined Eston in Ohio when mounting tensions in the South increased the danger of being targeted by slave catchers or vigilantes. Sally's runaway children, son Beverly and daughter Harriet, disappeared into the white communities of their spouses.

In an 1805 letter, Jefferson wrote of his disillusionment with the possibility that emancipation would be brought about in his day.

I have long since given up the expectation of any early provision for the extinguishment of slavery among us. There are many virtuous men who would make any sacrifices to effect it. many equally virtuous who persuade themselves either that the thing is not wrong, or that it cannot be remedied. and very many with whom interest is morality. the older we grow, the larger we are disposed to believe the last party to be. but interest is really going over to the side of morality. [75]

He did not count himself among those virtuous men. The record of his life rather suggests he belonged to the group that considered slavery a problem that could not be remedied. But he could have remedied it in his own life. When we consider how doggedly he pursued every other cause he ever fought for, his protestations that he wished as strongly as any for the remedy rings hollow.

Jefferson kept his promise to Sally Hemings, but it was all he could afford. He died owing $107,000 to creditors. Though some of this debt had been inherited, and $20,000 undertaken due to his co-signing of a loan, much was due to Jefferson's own spending habits. He kept a fully stocked and generously opened wine cellar, was a lifelong collector of books (he sold 6487 to the new Library of Congress), and sank huge sums into Monticello's construction and decoration. The mansion was auctioned off, as were 140 slaves. The house would be redeemed in 1923, when it was purchased by the Thomas Jefferson Foundation. Slavery, of course, would continue in Virginia until the Civil War.

There is no simple way to separate the works of Thomas Jefferson from the man himself. As a champion of liberty he devoted half his life to relieving persons of his own class from the burdens of monarchical domination. And despite not working directly to elevate the status of those in the lowest echelons of social hierarchy, his ideas inspired generations of politicians to promote equality as American democracy's end goal. Both Abraham Lincoln and Martin Luther King Jr., among many others, evoked the Declaration of Independence as proof that the United States had been founded on principles that required a radical re-alignment of social order. That Jefferson himself had not made abolition one of his goals is a tragedy, because of all the influential figures of the Revolutionary period, he was the best equipped to see it through to a peaceful conclusion.

Great acts do not require great men to enact them, but when a man such as Jefferson wrings greatness from everything he turns his hand to, we cannot deny him that label. Jefferson was an exemplary thinker and politician. His scholarship, productivity, and the devotion he showed to his family and friends are worthy of the highest admiration. Examining his failings is worthwhile because it reminds us that even the truly great are liable to err due to cultural bias, self-interest, and simple ignorance. His achievements inspire us to ask what we ourselves might achieve. From his failings we take warning. If one blessed with all the advantages of mind and education that nature and man can bestow could leave himself open to history's censure, how much more strenuously must we exert ourselves "to follow truth wherever it may lead, nor to tolerate any error so long as reason is left free to combat it"? [76]

References
2. A Long Shadow

[1] http://www.surveyhistory.org/peter_jefferson1.htm

[2] http://www.encyclopediavirginia.org/Fry-Jefferson_Map_of_Virginia

[3] Meacham, Jon. Thomas Jefferson the Art of Power. New York: Random House, 2012. Print.

[4] Beran, Michael Knox. Jefferson's Demons: Portrait of a Restless Mind. Free, 2003. Print.

[5] "Thomas Jefferson to Dabney Carr, 19 January 1816," Founders Online, National Archives (http://founders.archives.gov/documents/Jefferson/03-09-02-0238 [last update: 2015-12-30]). Source: The Papers of Thomas Jefferson, Retirement
Series, vol. 9, September 1815 to April 1816, ed. J. Jefferson Looney. Princeton: Princeton University Press, 2012, pp. 367–369.

3. Natural Distinctions

[6] http://www.heritage.org/initiatives/first-principles/primary-sources/jeffersons-first-inaugural-address

[7] "From Thomas Jefferson to William Fleming, 20 March 1764," Founders Online, National Archives (http://founders.archives.gov/documents/Jefferson/01-01-02-0009 [last update: 2015-12-30]). Source: The Papers of Thomas Jefferson, vol. 1, 1760–1776, ed. Julian P. Boyd. Princeton: Princeton University Press, 1950, pp. 15–17.

[8] http://www.pbs.org/wgbh/aia/part1/1h315t.html

[9] http://www.let.rug.nl/usa/presidents/thomas-jefferson/jefferson-on-slavery.php

[10] http://www.pbs.org/wgbh/aia/part2/2p84.html

[11] http://www.pbs.org/wgbh/aia/part2/2h71t.html

[12] http://www.pbs.org/wgbh/aia/part2/2h72t.htm

[13] "From Thomas Jefferson to Condorcet, 30 August 1791," Founders Online, National Archives (http://founders.archives.gov/documents/Jefferson/01-22-02-0092 [last update: 2015-12-30]). Source: The Papers of Thomas Jefferson, vol. 22, 6 August 1791 – 31 December 1791, ed. Charles T. Cullen. Princeton: Princeton University Press, 1986, pp. 98–99.

4. Liberty, Equality, Fraternity

[14] "Thomas Jefferson to Joel Barlow, 8 October 1809," Founders Online, National Archives (http://founders.archives.gov/documents/Jefferson/03-01-02-0461 [last update: 2015-12-30]). Source: The Papers of Thomas Jefferson, Retirement Series, vol. 1, 4 March 1809 to 15 November 1809, ed. J. Jefferson Looney. Princeton: Princeton University Press, 2004, pp. 588–590.

[15] "III. Jefferson's "original Rough draught" of the Declaration of Independence, 11 June–4 July 1776," Founders Online, National Archives (http://founders.archives.gov/documents/Jefferson/01-01-02-0176-0004 [last update: 2015-12-30]).
Source: The Papers of Thomas Jefferson, vol. 1, 1760–1776, ed. Julian P. Boyd. Princeton: Princeton University Press, 1950, pp. 423–428.
[16]"79. A Bill for the More General Diffusion of Knowledge, 18 June 1779," Founders Online, National Archives (http://founders.archives.gov/documents/Jefferson/01-02-02-0132-0004-0079 [last update: 2015-12-30]). Source: The Papers of Thomas Jefferson, vol. 2, 1777 – 18 June 1779, ed. Julian P. Boyd. Princeton: Princeton University Press, 1950, pp. 526–535.
Jefferson, vol. 2, 1777 – 18 June 1779, ed. Julian P. Boyd. Princeton: Princeton University Press, 1950, pp. 545–553.
[18] http://www.encyclopediavirginia.org/_Life_of_

Isaac_Jefferson_of_Petersburg_Virginia_Blacksmith_by_Isaac_Jefferson_1847

5. The Other Women

[19] "From Thomas Jefferson to Maria Cosway, 12 October 1786," Founders Online, National Archives (http://founders.archives.gov/documents/Jefferson/01-10-02-0309 [last update: 2015-12-30]). Source: The Papers of Thomas Jefferson, vol. 10, 22 June–31 December 1786, ed. Julian P. Boyd. Princeton: Princeton University Press, 1954, pp. 443–455.

6. The Winter Pilgrim

[20] "From Thomas Jefferson to Chastellux, 4 April 1787," Founders Online, National Archives (http://founders.archives.gov/documents/Jefferson/01-11-02-0255 [last update: 2015-12-30]). Source: The Papers of Thomas Jefferson, vol. 11, 1 January–6 August 1787, ed. Julian P. Boyd. Princeton: Princeton University Press, 1955, pp.

261–262.

[21] http://www.let.rug.nl/usa/presidents/thomas-jefferson/letters-of-thomas-jefferson/jefl79.php

[22] "From Thomas Jefferson to John Jay, 19 July 1789," Founders Online, National Archives (http://founders.archives.gov/documents/Jefferson/01-15-02-0277 [last update: 2015-12-30]). Source: The Papers of Thomas Jefferson, vol. 15, 27 March 1789 – 30 November 1789, ed. Julian P. Boyd. Princeton: Princeton University Press, 1958, pp. 284–291.

[23] "To Thomas Jefferson from Lafayette, [25 August 1789]," Founders Online, National Archives (http://founders.archives.gov/documents/Jefferson/01-15-02-0349 [last update: 2015-12-30]). Source: The Papers of Thomas Jefferson, vol. 15, 27 March 1789 – 30 November 1789, ed. Julian P. Boyd. Princeton: Princeton University Press, 1958, pp. 354–355.

[24] "From Thomas Jefferson to Maria Cosway,

[5 October 1786]," Founders Online, National Archives (http://founders.archives.gov/documents/Jefferson/01-10-02-0297 [last update: 2015-12-30]). Source: The Papers of Thomas Jefferson, vol. 10, 22 June–31 December 1786, ed. Julian P. Boyd. Princeton: Princeton University Press, 1954, pp. 431–433.

8. Duty and Domesticity

[25] "From Thomas Jefferson to George Washington, 15 December 1789," Founders Online, National Archives (http://founders.archives.gov/documents/Jefferson/01-16-02-0026 [last update: 2015-12-30]). Source: The Papers of Thomas Jefferson, vol. 16, 30 November 1789–4 July 1790, ed. Julian P. Boyd. Princeton: Princeton University Press, 1961, pp. 34–35.

9. A Divided House

[26] "X. Jefferson's Account of the Bargain on the Assumption and Residence Bills, [1792?],"

Founders Online, National Archives (http://founders.archives.gov/documents/Jefferson/01-17-02-0018-0012 [last update: 2015-12-30]). Source: The Papers of Thomas Jefferson, vol. 17, 6 July–3 November 1790, ed. Julian P. Boyd. Princeton: Princeton University Press, 1965, pp. 205–208.

[27] "Opinion on the Constitutionality of the Bill for Establishing a National Bank, 15 February 1791," Founders Online, National Archives (http://founders.archives.gov/documents/Jefferson/01-19-02-0051 [last update: 2015-12-30]). Source: The Papers of Thomas Jefferson, vol. 19, 24 January–31 March 1791, ed. Julian P. Boyd. Princeton: Princeton University Press, 1974, pp. 275–282.

[28] "Final Version of an Opinion on the Constitutionality of an Act to Establish a Bank, [23 February 1791]," Founders Online, National Archives (http://founders.archives.gov/documents/Hamilton/01-08-02-0060-0003 [last update: 2015-12-

30]). Source: The Papers of Alexander Hamilton, vol. 8, February 1791 – July 1791, ed. Harold C. Syrett. New York: Columbia University Press, 1965, pp. 97–134.

10. A War of Words

[29] John Adams, The Works of John Adams, Second President of the United States: with a Life of the Author, Notes and Illustrations, by his Grandson Charles Francis Adams (Boston: Little, Brown and Co., 1856). 10 volumes. Vol. 6. 1/8/2016.
<http://oll.libertyfund.org/titles/2104>
[30]
http://www.constitution.org/cmt/freneau/republic2monarchy.htm
[31] John Adams, Discourses on Davila : a series of papers, on political history. Written in the year 1790, and then published in the Gazette of the United States / by an American citizen. (Boston : Russell and Cutler, 1805). (http://www.johnadamslibrary.org/book/?book=2100634Adams%20170.11)

[32] http://www.loc.gov/teachers/classroommaterials/connections/thomas-jefferson/history5.html

[33] "From Thomas Jefferson to William Short, 3 January 1793," Founders Online, National Archives (http://founders.archives.gov/documents/Jefferson/01-25-02-0016 [last update: 2015-12-30]). Source: The Papers of Thomas Jefferson, vol. 25, 1 January–10 May 1793, ed. John Catanzariti. Princeton: Princeton University Press, 1992, pp. 14–17.

[34] "From Thomas Jefferson to Martha Jefferson Randolph, 28 April 1793," Founders Online, National Archives (http://founders.archives.gov/documents/Jefferson/01-25-02-0566 [last update: 2015-12-30]). Source: The Papers of Thomas Jefferson, vol. 25, 1 January–10 May 1793, ed. John Catanzariti. Princeton: Princeton University Press, 1992, pp. 621–622.

11. The Farmer's Son

[35] "From Thomas Jefferson to James Madison, 9 June 1793," Founders Online, National Archives (http://founders.archives.gov/documents/Jefferson/01-26-02-0219 [last update: 2015-12-30]). Source: The Papers of Thomas Jefferson, vol. 26, 11 May–31 August 1793, ed. John Catanzariti. Princeton: Princeton University Press, 1995, pp. 239–242.

[36] https://www.monticello.org/site/plantation-and-slavery/nailery

[37] https://www.monticello.org/site/plantation-and-slavery/robert-hemings

[38] https://history.state.gov/milestones/1784-1800/jay-treaty

12. Crimes and Punishments

[39] http://www.ourdocuments.gov/doc.php?doc=16&page=transcript

[40] "From Thomas Jefferson to Thomas Mann

Randolph, 9 May 1798," Founders Online, National Archives (http://founders.archives.gov/documents/Jefferson/01-30-02-0238 [last update: 2015-12-30]). Source: The Papers of Thomas Jefferson, vol. 30, 1 January 1798 – 31 January 1799, ed. Barbara B. Oberg. Princeton: Princeton University Press, 2003, pp. 341–342.

[41] https://www.libraries.psu.edu/psul/digital/pahistory/folder_3.html

[42] http://www.fjc.gov/history/home.nsf/page/tu_sedbio_lyon.html

[43] http://www.fjc.gov/history/home.nsf/page/tu_sedition_hd_jc_indictment.html

[44] "III. Resolutions Adopted by the Kentucky General Assembly, 10 November 1798," Founders Online, National Archives (http://founders.archives.gov/documents/Jefferson/01-30-02-0370-0004 [last update: 2015-12-30]). Source: The Papers of

Thomas Jefferson, vol. 30, 1 January 1798 – 31 January 1799, ed. Barbara B. Oberg. Princeton: Princeton University Press

[45] "To Thomas Jefferson from Martha Jefferson Randolph, 22 January 1798," Founders Online, National Archives (http://founders.archives.gov/documents/Jefferson/01-30-02-0028 [last update: 2015-12-30]). Source: The Papers of Thomas Jefferson, vol. 30, 1 January 1798 – 31 January 1799, ed. Barbara B. Oberg. Princeton: Princeton University Press, 2003, pp. 43–44.

[46] "Thomas Jefferson to Walter Jones, 2 January 1814," Founders Online, National Archives (http://founders.archives.gov/documents/Jefferson/03-07-02-0052 [last update: 2015-12-30]). Source: The Papers of Thomas Jefferson, Retirement Series, vol. 7, 28 November 1813 to 30 September 1814, ed. J. Jefferson Looney. Princeton: Princeton University Press, 2010, pp. 100–104."Thomas Jefferson to Walter Jones, 2

January 1814," Founders Online, National Archives (http://founders.archives.gov/documents/Jefferson/03-07-02-0052 [last update: 2015-12-30]). Source: The Papers of Thomas Jefferson, Retirement Series, vol. 7, 28 November 1813 to 30 September 1814, ed. J. Jefferson Looney. Princeton: Princeton University Press, 2010, pp. 100–104.

[47] http://www.encyclopediavirginia.org/gabriel_s_conspiracy_1800#start_entry

[48] Egerton, Douglas R.. Gabriel's rebellion: the Virginia slave conspiracies of 1800 and 1802. University of North Carolina Press, 1993

[49] "From Thomas Jefferson to James Monroe, 20 September 1800," Founders Online, National Archives (http://founders.archives.gov/documents/Jefferson/01-32-02-0097 [last update: 2015-12-30]). Source: The Papers of Thomas Jefferson, vol. 32, 1 June 1800 – 16 February 1801, ed. Barbara B. Oberg. Princeton: Princeton

13. Strange Bedfellows

[50] "Letter from Alexander Hamilton, Concerning the Public Conduct and Character of John Adams, Esq. President of the United States, [24 October 1800]," Founders Online, National Archives (http://founders.archives.gov/documents/Hamilton/01-25-02-0110-0002 [last update: 2015-12-30]). Source: The Papers of Alexander Hamilton, vol. 25, July 1800 – April 1802, ed. Harold C. Syrett. New York: Columbia University Press, 1977,
pp. 186–234.

[51] "From Alexander Hamilton to Theodore Sedgwick, 10 May 1800," Founders Online, National Archives (http://founders.archives.gov/documents/Hamilton/01-24-02-0387 [last update: 2015-12-30]). Source: The Papers of Alexander Hamilton, vol. 24, November 1799 – June 1800, ed. Harold C. Syrett. New York: Columbia University

Press, 1976, pp. 474–475.

[52] http://www.theatlantic.com/magazine/archive/2004/03/how-jefferson-counted-himself-in/302888/

[53] "From Alexander Hamilton to James A. Bayard, 16 January 1801," Founders Online, National Archives (http://founders.archives.gov/documents/Hamilton/01-25-02-0169 [last update: 2015-12-30]). Source: The Papers of Alexander Hamilton, vol. 25, July 1800 – April 1802, ed. Harold C. Syrett. New York: Columbia University Press, 1977, pp. 319–324.

[54] "III. First Inaugural Address, 4 March 1801," Founders Online, National Archives (http://founders.archives.gov/documents/Jefferson/01-33-02-0116-0004 [last update: 2015-12-30]). Source: The Papers of Thomas Jefferson, vol. 33, 17 February–30 April 1801, ed. Barbara B. Oberg. Princeton: Princeton University Press, 2006, pp. 148–152.

14. Triumphs and Tribulations, Part One

[55] https://history.state.gov/milestones/1801-1829/barbary-wars

[56] https://www.monticello.org/site/research-and-collections/first-barbary-war

[57] Dudley W. Knox, ed. (1939). Naval Documents related to the United States Wars with the Barbary Powers, Volume I. Washington: United States Government Printing Office.

[58] "From Thomas Jefferson to Thomas Mann Randolph, 12 March 1801," Founders Online, National Archives (http://founders.archives.gov/documents/Jefferson/01-33-02-0220 [last update: 2015-12-30]). Source: The Papers of Thomas Jefferson, vol. 33, 17 February–30 April 1801, ed. Barbara B. Oberg. Princeton: Princeton University Press, 2006, pp. 259–260.

[59] "From Thomas Jefferson to Mary Jefferson Eppes, 3 March 1802," Founders Online, National Archives (http://founders.archives.gov/documents/Jeffer

son/01-36-02-0450 [last update: 2015-12-30]). Source: The Papers of Thomas Jefferson, vol. 36, 1 December 1801–3 March 1802, ed. Barbara B. Oberg. Princeton: Princeton University Press, 2009, pp. 676–677.

15. The Case of Thomas Jefferson and Sally Hemings

[60] "From James Madison to James Monroe, 1 June 1801," Founders Online, National Archives (http://founders.archives.gov/documents/Madison/02-01-02-0321 [last update: 2015-12-30]). Source: The Papers of James Madison, Secretary of State
Series, vol. 1, 4 March–31 July 1801, ed. Robert J. Brugger, Robert A. Rutland, Robert Rhodes Crout, Jeanne K. Sisson, and Dru Dowdy. Charlottesville: University Press of Virginia, 1986, pp. 244–246.

[61] The Recorder; or, Lady's and Gentleman's Miscellany, September 1, 1802, 2; Barbara B. Oberg, ed., The Papers of Thomas Jefferson (Princeton, NJ: Princeton University Press,

2012), 38:323–325.

[62] "´Life among the Lowly, No. 1," Pike County (Ohio) Republican, March 13, 1873.

17. A Failure of Ideals

[63] http://etc.usf.edu/lit2go/132/presidential-addresses-and-messages/5165/second-inaugural-address-washington-dc-march-4-1805/

[64] "From Thomas Jefferson to William DuVal, 22 June 1806," Founders Online, National Archives (http://founders.archives.gov/documents/Jefferson/99-01-02-3887 [last update: 2015-12-30]). Source: this is an Early Access document from The
Papers of Thomas Jefferson. It is not an authoritative final version.

[65] "From Thomas Jefferson to United States Congress, 22 January 1807," Founders Online, National Archives (http://founders.archives.gov/documents/Jefferson/99-01-02-4925 [last update: 2015-12-30]).

Source: this is an Early Access document from The Papers of Thomas Jefferson. It is not an authoritative final version.

[66] "From Thomas Jefferson to William Thomson, 26 September 1807," Founders Online, National Archives (http://founders.archives.gov/documents/Jefferson/99-01-02-6452 [last update: 2015-12-30]). Source: this is an Early Access document from The Papers of Thomas Jefferson. It is not an authoritative final version.

[67] "To Thomas Jefferson from Albert Gallatin, 18 December 1807," Founders Online, National Archives (http://founders.archives.gov/documents/Jefferson/99-01-02-7020 [last update: 2015-12-30]). Source: this is an Early Access document from The Papers of Thomas Jefferson. It is not an authoritative final version.

18. The Finished Legacy

[68] "Proclamation on the Embargo, 19 April 1808," Founders Online, National Archives

(http://founders.archives.gov/documents/Jefferson/99-01-02-7862 [last update: 2015-12-30]). Source: this is an Early Access document from The Papers of
Thomas Jefferson. It is not an authoritative final version.

[69] "From Thomas Jefferson to John Taylor, 6 January 1808," Founders Online, National Archives (http://founders.archives.gov/documents/Jefferson/99-01-02-7143 [last update: 2015-12-30]). Source: this is an Early Access document from The
Papers of Thomas Jefferson. It is not an authoritative final version.

[70] http://www.pbs.org/wgbh/pages/frontline/shows/jefferson/cron/1868randall.html

[71] "Thomas Jefferson to Benjamin Rush, 5 December 1811," Founders Online, National Archives (http://founders.archives.gov/documents/Jefferson/03-04-02-0248 [last update: 2015-12-30]).

Source: The Papers of Thomas Jefferson, Retirement Series, vol. 4, 18 June 1811 to 30 April 1812, ed. J. Jefferson Looney. Princeton: Princeton University Press, 2007, pp. 312–314.

[72] "Thomas Jefferson to John Adams, 22 August 1813," Founders Online, National Archives (http://founders.archives.gov/documents/Jefferson/03-06-02-0351 [last update: 2015-12-30]). Source: The Papers of Thomas Jefferson, Retirement Series, vol. 6, 11 March to 27 November 1813, ed. J. Jefferson Looney. Princeton: Princeton University Press, 2009, pp. 438–441.

19. A Great Man

[73] https://www.monticello.org/site/jefferson/deathbed-adieu

[74] "From Thomas Jefferson to John Holmes, 22 April 1820," Founders Online, National Archives

(http://founders.archives.gov/documents/Jefferson/98-01-02-1234 [last update: 2015-12-30]). Source: this is an Early Access document from The
Papers of Thomas Jefferson: Retirement Series. It is not an authoritative final version.

[75] "From Thomas Jefferson to William Armistead Burwell, 28 January 1805," Founders Online, National Archives (http://founders.archives.gov/documents/Jefferson/99-01-02-1057 [last update: 2015-12-30]). Source: this is an Early Access document from The Papers of Thomas Jefferson. It is not an authoritative final version.

[76] "From Thomas Jefferson to William Roscoe, 27 December 1820," Founders Online, National Archives (http://founders.archives.gov/documents/Jefferson/98-01-02-1712 [last update: 2015-12-30]). Source: this is an Early Access document From The Papers of Thomas Jefferson: Retirement Series. It is not an authoritative final version.

Made in the USA
Middletown, DE
29 May 2018